THE FISHERMAN'S GUIDE TO TACKLE

THE FISHERMAN'S
GUIDE TO
TACKLE

ESSENTIAL HINTS, TACTICS AND TECHNIQUES

EMILIO
FERNÁNDEZ
ROMÁN

SWAN·HILL
PRESS

British Library Cataloguing-in-Publication Data
A catalogue record for this book
is available from the British Library

ISBN 1 85310 056 4

Typeset by Rowland Phototypesetting Ltd, Bury St Edmunds, Suffolk
Printed in England by St Edmundsbury Press Ltd, Bury St Edmunds, Suffolk

Swan Hill Press
an imprint of Airlife Publishing Ltd
101 Longden Road, Shrewsbury, SY3 9EB, England

Contents

CONTENTS

9

CONTENTS

THE FISHERMAN'S
GUIDE TO
TACKLE

1. FISHING IN GENERAL

LINE CONTROL

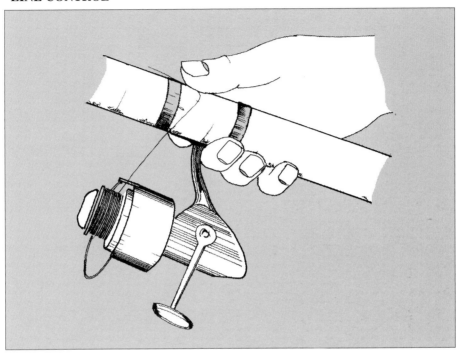

When casting with a fixed spool reel on cold days, when your fingers may be numb or gloved and less sensitive, it can be easier to control the line with your thumb, as shown.

WEIGHTS

A selection of easily interchangeable weights of various sizes can be made by cutting small rectangles of soft sheet metal (but not lead, for environmental reasons) that can be doubled over and pinched onto the line.

TESTING HOOK SHARPNESS

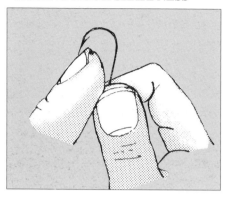

To check the sharpness and penetration of a hook point, press it at an angle against a fingernail. If it slips along it is not sharp enough. This may be put right if you can sharpen it quickly with a pocket sharpener. If not, use another sharper hook.

PIKE FISHING

When pike are your quarry, irrespective of the particular method or tackle you intend to use, it is important to go equipped with a good selection of extra hooks, traces, lures and baits.

TROUT LINES

Trout can and will lie at all kinds of depths, in the shallows or the very deepest holes. Where they are actually to be found on a particular day and in a particular stretch of water depends upon an angler's ability to 'read the water' and make a careful reconnaissance.

LINE BREAKING-STRAIN

Choosing the correct test strength of line is always something of a challenge. A good rule of thumb is to use a line with a test strength that is twice the weight of the average fish for that stretch of water, and go up to three times where there is a lot of aquatic vegetation.

WATER DEPTH

Controlling the depth at which your line fishes can be done by careful angling of the rod. A high rod point will tend to make the line ride high in the water, while a low angle will cause the line to fish deeper.

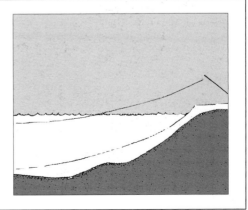

HANGING WEIGHTS

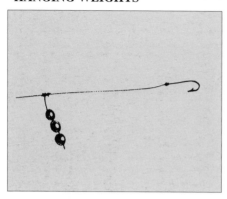

When fishing with a natural bait such as a worm or maggot, it is a good idea to have weights fixed to a dropper, or otherwise offset from the main line. If a snag occurs, only the weights may be lost; it is easier to detect a fish's take; and the bait can be trotted more easily over underwater obstacles.

FLOATS

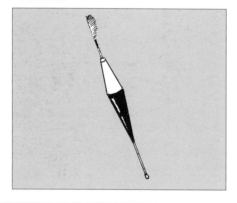

At certain hours of the day, such as when you are squinting into bright sunshine, it can be difficult to see a float unless it stands quite high above the water. When inserted into the top of the float, a small feather, (preferably of a light colour) can greatly assist matters.

FIXED SPOOL REELS AND LINES

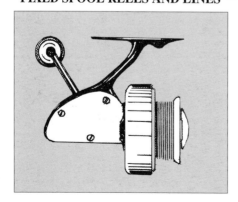

Whatever the size or capacity of a particular fixed spool reel, it will cast furthest and most accurately if it carries the correct bulk of line – not too little, nor too much. For best results, the line should fill the spool to slightly less than its maximum capacity.

THE BALANCE OF FLOATS

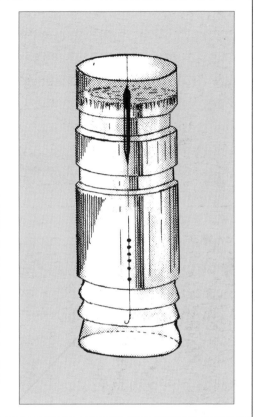

Whatever type of fish you are pursuing, float fishing is most successful when the float is correctly balanced to ride at the desired height in the water, and upright. Perhaps the best and simplest way to test the characteristics of each of your floats, when tackled up with hook(s) and weight(s), is to use a large, clear plastic bottle such as is used for mineral water and various other liquids, having first cut off the shoulder and neck.

MINIMUM FISH LENGTHS

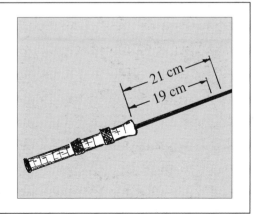

Where fishery rules require that fish under certain minimum lengths must be returned to the water, it is useful to have a selection of length markers painted on the butt section of the rod, just above the handle.

FISHING TACTICS

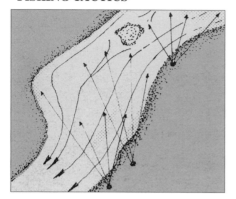

It is wise to fish a piece of water methodically and thoughtfully, starting with the nearer sections and gradually extending your casting to cover further stretches. It is usually necessary to change the speed and depth at which the line is fishing, to achieve full coverage of the water. Where possible, it is usually preferable to fish upstream, approaching lying fish from behind.

FREEING A SNAGGED LINE

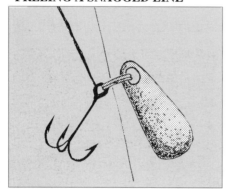

A fairly large treble hook, connected by a split ring to a weight of about 56.7 g (2 oz), will serve as a simple and effective tool for freeing a hook stuck in an underwater obstacle. Slip the fishing line through the split ring so that the weight and treble hook can be allowed to run freely down the line, attached to their own strong recovery cord or heavy line.

NYLON

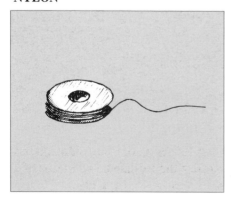

Do you realise that monofilament nylon line is highly vulnerable to the sun's ultraviolet rays? Exposure to daylight will quickly weaken a line and lost fish may be the disappointing result. Keep spools of monofilament line out of direct sunlight, and discard any that have been subjected to bright sunlight.

FISH LIES IN STILL WATERS

In lakes and reservoirs, fish lies are influenced by underwater currents and contours, and the larger, more cautious fish will often lie deeper than their more naïve little cousins. Where a marginal shelf drops away into deeper water is often a rewarding place to seek the bigger specimens.

SECURING A LINE

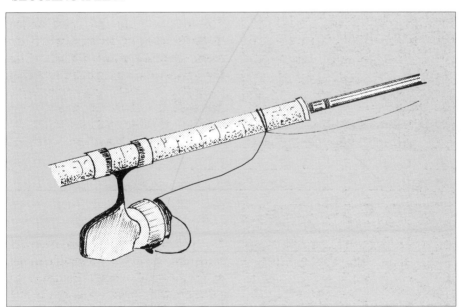

When fishing with a fixed length of line, when ledgering or using a float, it is a good tip to have the line held very gently against the rod handle by means of a rubber band. If a fish takes, it will be aware of little or no resistance.

WEIGHING A FISH

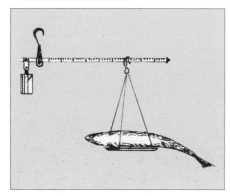

A steelyard-type balance is a very simple, ancient but accurate means of weighing a fish. It is an easy and interesting matter to make one yourself, with a long arm and a counterbalance, and using various objects of known weight to calibrate and mark off the arm at intervals to indicate pounds and ounces, or kilos and kilograms.

SWIVELS THAT SWIVEL!

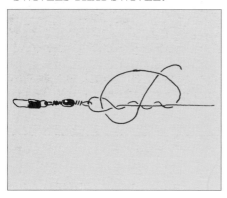

Few bits of tackle are more useless than swivels that do not rotate, causing the line to twist and kink. Wash a new swivel thoroughly in warm soapy water. Rinse and dry it thoroughly, and apply a tiny drop of viscous oil or very light grease to the central spindle or shank of the swivel.

"POPPING CORK"

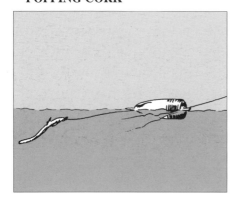

We usually associate the "popper" with the use of artificial lures for Black bass, but the full term is the "popping cork", referring to the use of cork or other buoyant material to support a bait. It is extremely useful when Black bass are the quarry, and the underside of the float must be concave if it is to work correctly.

WEIGHTS FOR CARP FISHING

A very reliable tackle set-up for carp is shown in this drawing. Use a suitable weight with the line running freely through a good-sized ring, so that the line has the maximum freedom to run easily.

WATER TEMPERATURE

A thermometer can be a useful aid in deciding the best lures and baits for trout fishing, as the fish and their food species are all greatly influenced by the water temperature. In general, a worm – perhaps fished by the very skilful upstream method – will fare best if the water is not more than 12°C (53.6°F). The wet fly or nymph is preferable at temperatures in the range 12°C–16°C (53.6–60.8°F), and the dry fly when it is warmer.

REMOVING SPLIT SHOT

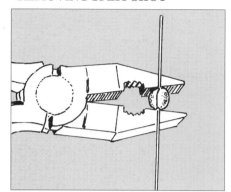

Sometimes it can be difficult to remove small split weights without the risk of weakening or cutting the line. A reliable method is to use a small pair of pliers or pincers with fairly fine jaws, and to squeeze gently but firmly in line with the slot in the weight. Pressure applied in this way will cause the slot to open up and release its grip on the line.

DRYING OUT WADERS

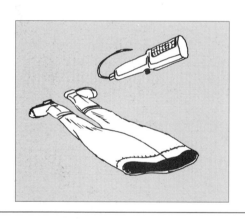

Because they retain the warmth and perspiration from feet and legs, waders and fishing boots often become clammy and damp inside after a long day's fishing. The best drying-out method, far preferable to older tricks such as crumpled newspapers and suchlike, is to use one of the various electrical boot driers that are now available. These gently warm the boots, and moisture soon evaporates, leaving them dry and pleasant to wear the next day.

HOOK SHARPNESS

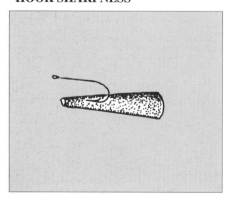

The difference between a fish in the net and a lost fish often boils down to the sharpness of the hook point. These should always be kept as sharp and straight as possible, and an essential part of each angler's equipment should be a small sharpening stone, with a fine-grain abrasive and shaped so as to be applied to even the tiniest hook.

BAIT FEEDER

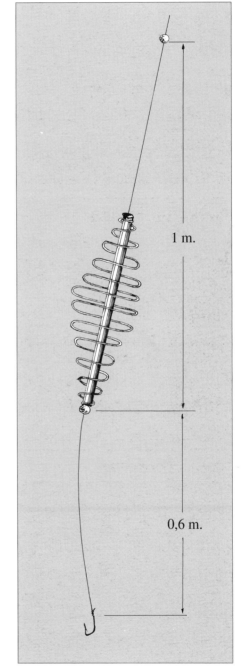

For bottom-feeding fish such as carp and tench, it is important to get tempting groundbait down to where the fish are feeding, which can be done by various means. One method well worth trying, and which can be simply and quickly made at home, is a container made from a spiral of wire formed around a central tube, as in the illustration. This can be slipped onto the line, and allowed to move up and down within a limited range by a shot pinched onto the line above and below it. Any soft bait such as bread, cheese, mixtures of gentles and other confections can easily be squeezed into the feeder spiral and moulded around the tube. Once the tackle is in the water, the contents of the spiral will leak out gradually.

ESTIMATING A FISH'S WEIGHT

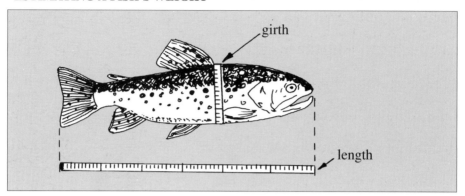

A formula exists for calculating the weight of a fish in the absence of any weighing scales. This is derived from an assessment of the fish's girth in relation to its overall length, and involves measuring the maximum girth, squaring the result, and multiplying it by the length. The result is then divided by 25, to give the weight. Thus the formula is $G^2 \times L \div 25$.

If we catch a trout with a girth of 22 cm (8.7 in) and a length of 36 cm (14.2 in), its weight in grams will be $22 \times 22 \times 36 \div 25 = 696$. We can conveniently round this up to 700 g (24.7 oz). This formula has been found to be accurate to within 5 per cent.

SPINNING LURES

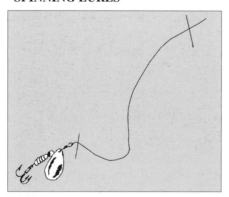

When fishing with any lure that spins, particular twisting stresses are placed on the last 25.4–38.1 cm (10–15 in) of a monofilament line. With repeated casting and retrieving, this can lead to tangles and eventual weakening of the all-important end of the line. It is therefore prudent to remove the spinning lure occasionally during the course of a long and active fishing day, cut off the final 30.5–45.7 cm (12–18 in) of monofilament, and attach the lure again. (Always dispose of unwanted lengths of line carefully, so that wildlife is not endangered by it.)

CATCH-AND-RELEASE HOOKS

Where fishery rules require fish to be released unharmed, or when you are likely to catch undersized or un-seasonable fish you will wish to return intact, it is a simple matter to convert a conventional barbed hook into one that is effectively barbless. A pair of fine-nosed pliers or pincers can be used to flatten the barb, as shown in the illustration, which then makes it a simple matter to slip the hook out of the mouth of any fish that is to be returned.

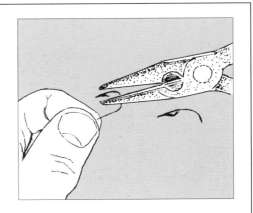

ROD LENGTH

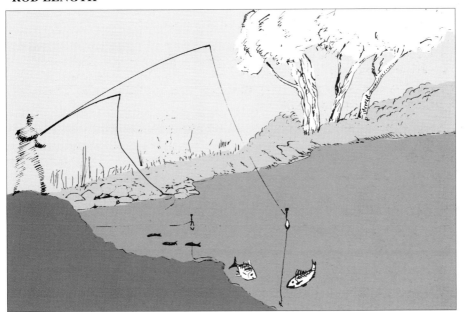

Particularly when fishing for carp and other bottom-living species in still-waters, a long rod gives obvious advantages. Once the line has been cast out, a rod that provides the angler with a long reach can be used to steer the line clear of marginal vegetation, allowing systematic coverage of the water in a way that is not possible with a very short rod.

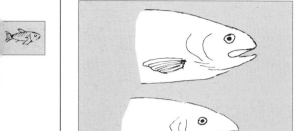

TROUT AND SALMON

It is fairly simple to tell the difference between salmon and trout, by examining the relative positions of the eye and the rear of the mandible. The rear extremity of a trout's mandible will extend to a point level with or beyond the centre or rear circumference of the eye, while that of a salmon reaches only to the forward edge of the eye.

TYPES OF TROUT

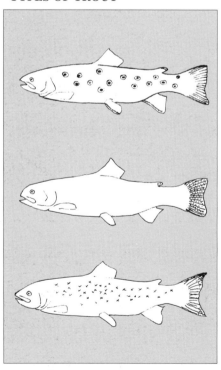

It is important to be able to distinguish between the three forms of trout that the average fisherman will encounter – the common brown trout, the migratory sea trout (both native) and the introduced rainbow trout.

Typically, the brown trout has orange or red spots on its flanks, and the adipose fin is fringed with the same colouring as the lines that are present on the fish's vental and anal fins.

The rainbow trout, frequently reared in hatcheries and fish farms for release into still waters, has a speckling of small black spots on its tail and adipose fin, and its flanks usually have the iridescent hue that gives the rainbow trout its name.

The sea trout is an anadromous fish, beginning its life in freshwater and migrating to the sea. It grows to maturity there, before returning to its home river to spawn. When freshly run in from the sea, it is easy to identify by its brilliant silver colouration and the presence on its flanks of dark spots, which look like small saltire crosses.

FISH ACTIVITY

Although there are many exceptions to general rules about fish behaviour, barometric pressure is often a good indicator as to the day's prospects for good sport, and a glance at your barometer is therefore well worthwhile. Typically, fish tend to be more active when the barometer indicates that pressure is dropping.

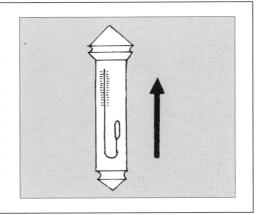

SMALL WEIGHTS

A spool of fuse-wire or fine solder can be a source of handy little homemade weights. When wrapped tightly around a core of piano wire with a loop formed at the top, a weight of any desired size can be quickly added directly to the line (as illustrated) or to a dropper.

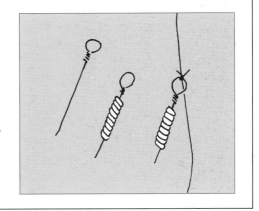

TACTICS

Typically, we cannot get any closer to a wild bird or other non-domesticated creature than the minimum distance at which it feels itself to be safe. The same applies to fish, especially trout. It therefore pays dividends for the angler to stay back from the water's edge, to avoid casting a shadow on the water or being skylined, and to keep a low profile, making use of whatever natural cover there may be.

A HINT ON ROD RINGS

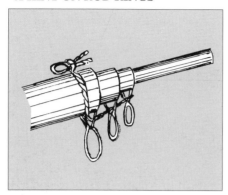

If you have a telescopic rod and wish to retract it to its minimum length, it is a good idea to do as shown in the illustration – using a length of cord, a twist of wire or, better still, a fluffy pipe-cleaner to secure the rings, so that the telescoped sections stay safely in place.

TAKING CARE OF FISH

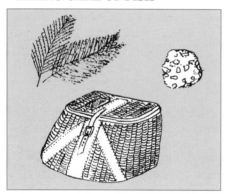

After they have been caught, we owe it to our fish to keep them in good condition. A creel or bass through which air can circulate freely is the best container, and it is useful to have a damp sponge in it, to maintain humidity. The old trick of placing fish on a bed of fresh vegetation is also a good one.

WIRE TRACES FOR PIKE FISHING

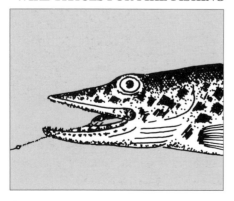

For pike fishing it is important to use a wire trace of about 15.2–22.9 cm (6–9 in) long between the end of the line and the hook. The pike – sometimes called the 'freshwater shark' – is equipped with a formidable mouthful of very sharp teeth, which can sever a monofilament line very quickly and easily.

PLAYING A FISH

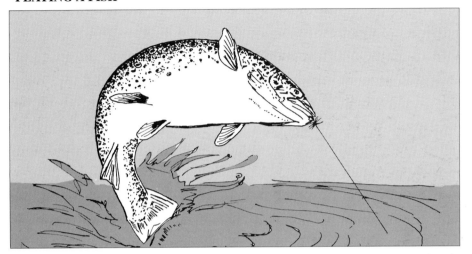

When it is being played, a fish's energies are worn down as its oxygen levels dwindle, a process that leads to its exhaustion through suffocation. Play a fish patiently, keeping it under firm tension but without subjecting it to excessive pressure.

NETTING A FISH

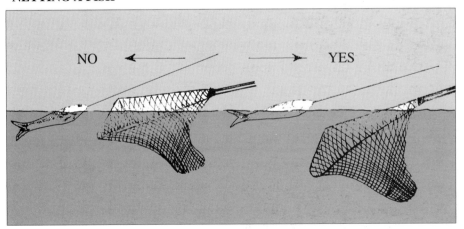

One of the most common ways in which a played-out fish is lost arises through bad handling of the landing net. The net should not be pushed like a shovel, to scoop the fish out of the water. Instead, it should be submerged and held steadily while the fish is drawn over it, and then raised promptly.

TROUT LIES

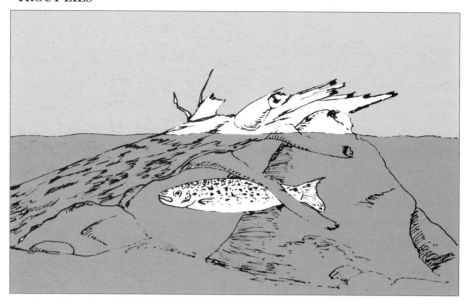

Trout always seek out good-sized lies, which afford a combination of shelter and security, room to move and a good food supply. These conditions often occur just behind a rock or other obstruction that interrupts the flow of a stream. Look out for such places when fishing a trout river.

FISH DISTRIBUTION

As a general rule, large fish spend most of their time quite deep in the water. Thus, a deeply-fished bait or lure will tend to be taken by larger fish than one which is fished close to the surface.

LUBRICATING ROD FERRULES

Graphite such as is found in the 'lead' of a pencil is an excellent dry lubricant, and helps to prevent rod ferrules from sticking. It is a simple matter to rub a soft-leaded pencil around the male unit of the joint, which deposits a coating that will make the sections easy to separate when the rod is taken down.

ALIGNING ROD-RINGS

When putting up a rod, it is important for the free running of the line that the rings are correctly lined up, and this means that the rod's sections must be correctly put together. Look carefully along the assembled rod to see that the rings are all in line. Small longitudinal painted marks above and below each joint also assist in achieving correct alignment each time a rod is put up.

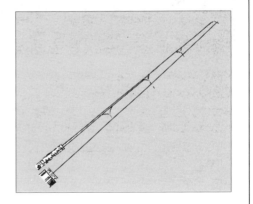

BAIT FEEDER

When angling for coarse fish, it is easy to make a feeder out of a plastic bottle or other similar container, that is especially effective in still-water fishing. A suitable weight, placed as in the illustration, will ensure it sinks fully.

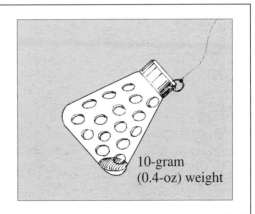

10-gram (0.4-oz) weight

BLACK BASS LIES

One of the most deadly techniques to use when fishing for black bass or black perch involves looking out for places where there are half-sunk branches or logs. Cast close to such places, and be ready for a take when the fly or lure is almost motionless.

LINE CHANGING

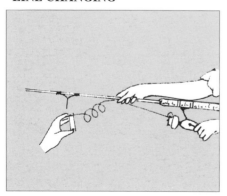

When it is time to wind a fresh spool of monofilament onto your reel, do it in such a way that the line winds off the spool and onto the reel without twisting. To smooth out kinks and twists, it is a good idea to have the line passing through the slight resistance of a pinched finger and thumb.

RELEASING TROUT

If you have to release a trout (perhaps because of fishery rules, or if it is undersized, or if you have caught enough), it is best to allow the fish to remain in the water, and not to touch it if possible. A barbless hook makes unhooking particularly easy, and can be removed smoothly. Fish that are not handled have a much better chance of survival.

EEL RIGS

Before setting out to fish for eels, it is wise to prepare a number of terminal tackle rigs that can be easily removed and changed. This means that when tangles or snags occur, no time is lost in recovering your only hook or swivel. A quick change and you are back in action.

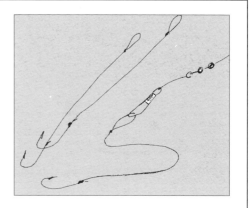

BANK FISHING

There is no getting away from the problems posed by bankside vegetation, which can overhang the water awkwardly and make access difficult. But never forget that these are also places of peace and safety for fish, and can therefore produce fine sport.

WHERE TO FISH FROM

Sometimes it is more productive to fish from the bank or shore than from a boat. The bank fisherman can make a careful study of the water's edge, spot the likely fish lies, and may often be able to present his fly or lure in the most natural way.

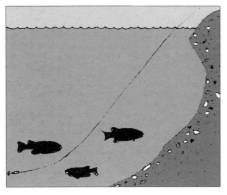

Towards the end of autumn, and especially into October, is a particularly good time to take good specimens of black bass, by fishing in areas of deep, dark water. Spoon lures and natural or synthetic worms can be equally effective.

2. BAIT FISHING

THE BAIT NEEDLE

Many anglers are surprisingly unfamiliar with the simple and extremely useful bait needle. This is a fine, pointed implement with an eyed end, which can be used to make the initial puncture in a worm or other bait, and then to draw in the hook, point foremost. Very small, light and cheap, it is a bait-fisher's essential tool.

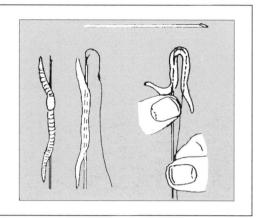

A PASTE-HOOK

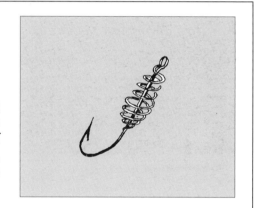

Paste-type bait can be made to cling more securely to the shank of the hook if it is moulded into a spiral of wire which has formed around it, from behind the eye back almost to the beginning of the bend.

GRASSHOPPERS AND CRICKETS

These are excellent natural baits, taken eagerly by trout, black bass and even barbel. A slice of bread coated with honey, syrup or other sweet spread can be left out towards dusk, covered loosely with a muslin cloth. By morning there should be a good harvest of baits for the day ahead.

A SPECIAL FLOAT

Deep Water
1. Where to make your cast
2. Cast again when float reaches here

Trout, like many other fish, prefer sheltered lies into which it can be very difficult to cast a bait. This challenge can often be best tackled with the use of a tiny float made from a spherical piece of polystyrene which has a slit in it to allow it to be fitted onto the line. The bait can then be cast (perhaps with a sideways movement) into the desired area. The little float makes a minimum of disturbance when it lands on the water; and the bait is presented in a convincing, natural way.

A LIVE-BAIT CONTAINER

A plastic can or container, pierced with a number of small holes in its upper parts and partly filled with water, can make a good live-bait container. If it is immersed in the river or lake, the water is constantly renewed through the little holes, keeping the baits well oxygenated and in good condition.

MOUNTING A DEAD BAIT

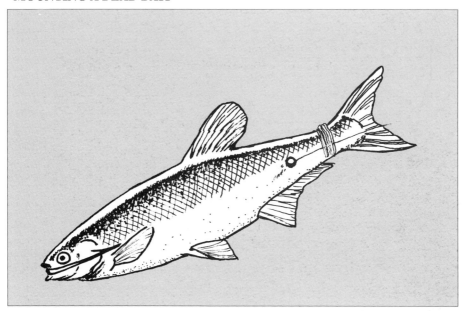

A dead bait, mounted as shown in the illustration, is one of the most successful methods when fishing in deep water. Setting it up like this is very simple – the line should be tied to the dead bait's body forward of the tail, before it enters the body and emerges at the mouth, where the hook is placed. A bait needle helps greatly in this procedure.

A BAIT BAG

A bag of fine mesh, such as the type used to hold oranges and other fruits, filled with fish-heads, guts and other scraps can be a good way of baiting a fishing spot, especially when sea fishing. It can be suspended in mid-water, or allowed to rest on the bottom. In the latter case some additional weight should be added as ballast.

'BOILIES'

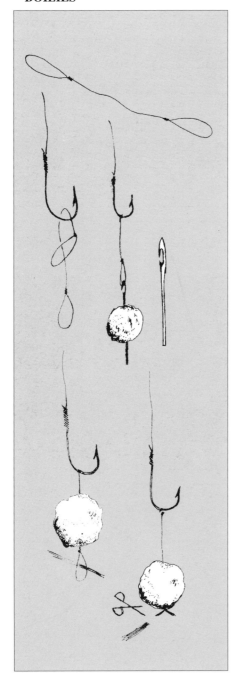

Some of the most productive baits for carp involve the use of balls of pre-cooked bait, a method first evolved in Britain and later adopted by French and Spanish coarse anglers. One of the best ways of mounting such baits involves the use of a crochet hook, as shown in this illustration. Pieces of knotted mono-filament or cotton hold the bait together, and if a ball of boiled bait should fall off into the water, that's all that is lost.

SECURING GRASSHOPPER BAITS

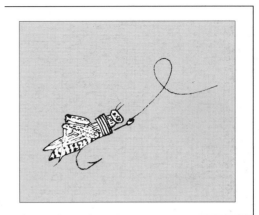

If grasshoppers or crickets are to be used as bait for trout (or barbel, which will also take them) the illustration shows the best and most secure way of mounting. It is always best to use a bait hook with a broad, flat area on top of the shank.

TROTTING WEIGHTS

When trotting a worm gently it is often unnecessary to use any additional weights. However, occasionally a strong current will make the use of weights essential to keep the bait fishing at a suitable depth. When this is necessary, small split weights should be added one by one to a dropper placed on the line a little above the bait, as shown in the illustration, until the correct weight and fishing depth is achieved.

A PRAWN OR SHRIMP MOUNT

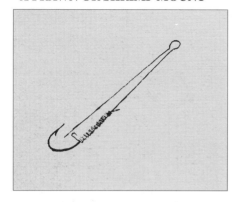

A special mount made of steel wire, as shown in this diagram, is a first-class device for mounting a shrimp or prawn bait. If an additionally secure mount is required, a few turns of fine monofilament line can be added.

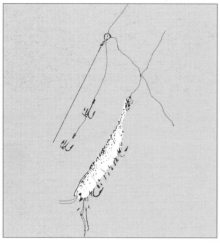

The second diagram shows a simple and easily-made rig for shrimp and prawn baits, which will hold the bait firmly even in vigorous casting, when other methods might allow it to fly off.

A FISH-FLY COMBINATION

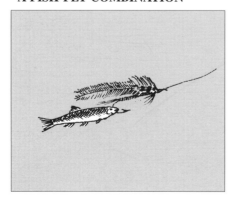

A highly attractive lure for black bass, and various other fish, involves the use of a long-winged or streamer-type fly lure, to which a tiny dead fish is fixed by hooking it through the upper and lower jaws. When cast along the water's edge and retrieved quite close in, this combination lure provides an attractive and effective combination of shape and erratic movement.

A LIVE-BAIT CONTAINER

This illustration shows a good set-up for keeping live-baits in good and active condition inside a metal container when you are travelling. The tube that runs into the upper part can be connected to the air intake of your car's engine. The partial vacuum it creates will cause air to be forced in through the tube that enters through the side of the container, thereby keeping the water oxygenated. It is important to tape up all joints firmly, so that the system is sealed and will work efficiently.

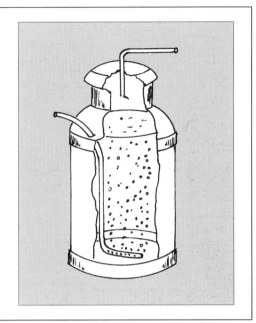

LAMPREYS

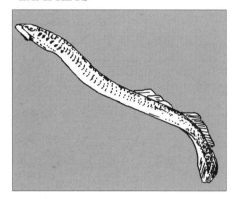

Lampreys are parasitic fish which attach themselves to their host fish by a circular sucker-like mouth, drawing nourishment from the host. Despite their rather repellent appearance, lampreys have long been regarded as a culinary delicacy. They can also be excellent natural baits.

DEEP-FISHING RIG

Many coarse fish such as tench are best fished for along the bottom, and the illustration shows a good rig for this type of angling. The weight and bait rest on the bottom, and when the fish takes, the float pops upright, having previously been lying horizontally on the surface of the water.

BAIT-FISHING ROD

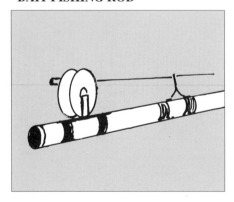

Fishing with a natural bait in places where there is a lot of waterside and aquatic vegetation is often made easier if a telescopic-type rod is used. Many bait-fishers prefer to use a free-running centre-pin reel such as is shown here.

LIKELY SPOTS

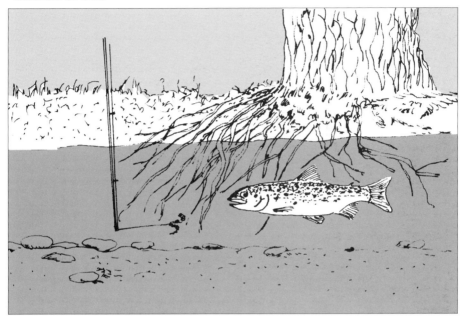

A likely type of place to find trout and other species is where a lie is created by underwater roots from bankside trees. When worming, the tip of the rod can be lowered into the water and the bait fed out to slip down with the current and into the reach of a fish lying in such a place.

3. BAITS

WORMING

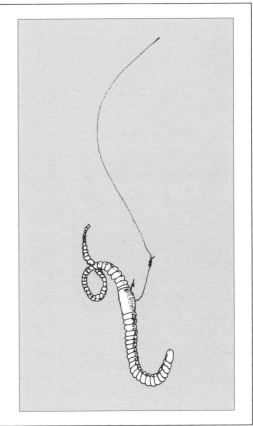

The simplest way of using a worm is to put it on a size 10 or 12 single hook, tied directly to the line. The worm should be hooked through the skin at its thickest point, which will give a secure hold while allowing the bait to wriggle freely and present a normal and attractive appearance to fish.

It is always best, if possible, to fish a worm freely with the current, without any weights to affect its movement. It will then move naturally as if it were just another worm being carried down by the stream. When a take is felt, wait for a brief moment before tightening into the fish.

DON'T WASTE WORMS

Why throw away any worms you have not used during your day's fishing? They can either be released into your garden, to improve the soil around plants and under the lawn, or kept alive and active in a pot filled with a moist mixture of soil and mulch.

DEAD-BAIT MOUNTING

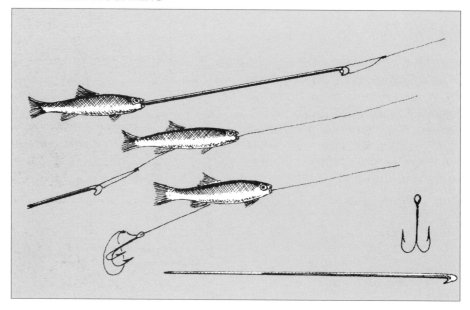

A baiting needle with a hooked end, as shown here, is a very useful implement for mounting dead-baits, allowing the loop-ended line to be threaded through the bait. The loop can then be quickly and easily used to attach a double or treble hook.

GRASSHOPPERS AND CRICKETS

These make fine baits, for trout as well as many species of coarse fish. Best results are usually obtained by fishing quite deep, and if light weights are pinched onto the line about 30 cm (12 in) above the hook, the bait will still be able to move fairly freely in the water.

GATHERING EARTHWORMS

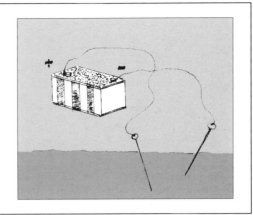

If conditions are mild and the ground moist, a quick way to gather earthworms is to stick two electrodes into the earth, one from each terminal of a car battery. Passing the current through the soil will bring worms to the surface.

BAIT TRAP

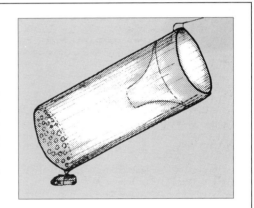

A one-litre (1.8-pint) plastic bottle can be easily modified as shown here, to make a good trap for minnows and other small bait-fish. It should be weighted at the bottom and have a recovery cord attached near the top.

WORMING RIG

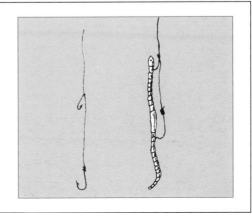

If a worm is correctly mounted it will behave naturally and last for some time. For a long worm, the rig shown here is a variation of the well-known Stewart system, which uses two single hooks of the same size.

LUGWORMS

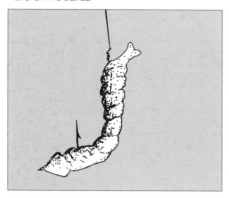

Lugworms are an excellent and favourite sea-fishing bait, and will keep well in a container holding moist sand or mud and strips of seaweed. Lugworms are readily found by digging in sand and mud at low tide.

DEAD-BAIT MOUNT

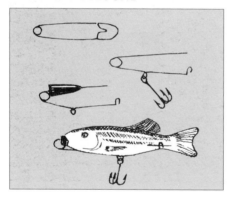

Here is an easy, quick and cheap way of making a good mount for a small dead-bait fish. All that is required is a safety-pin; the upper part of the cap of a ballpoint pen, with a small hole pierced in it; a small pair of pliers; a few moments of your time, and a little basic handiwork!

YOUR OWN MAGGOT FARM

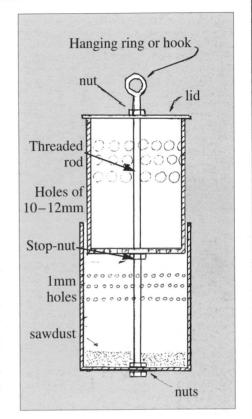

Hanging ring or hook

nut

lid

Threaded rod

Holes of 10–12mm

Stop-nut

1mm holes

sawdust

nuts

Here is a diagram of a small 'maggot farm' you can make quite easily out of two large empty paint tins. The upper section is pierced with a series of holes about 10–12 mm (0.4–0.5 in) in diameter to allow the flies to enter, while the lower section need have holes no more than a millimetre in diameter, to allow ventilation. In warm weather place scraps of raw meat in the upper section, and within a day or two you will find maggots in the lower part.

PIKE FISHING

A pike seizes its prey sideways, before turning it in its jaws and swallowing it. It therefore makes sense to have a hook placed somewhere along the middle of the bait, as well as towards the tail.

LIVE MAGGOTS

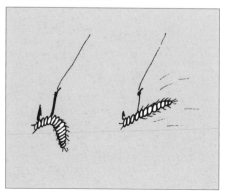

When fishing with live maggots, use very small, fine hooks. A maggot that is hooked lightly as illustrated will last well.

HERMIT CRABS

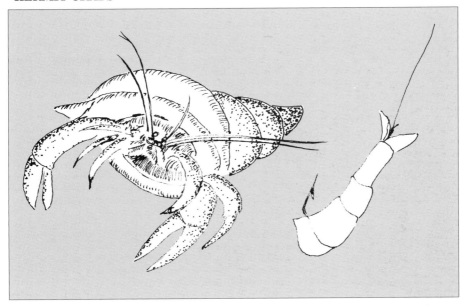

The hermit crab (often known simply as 'the hermit') is a very good bait for all forms of sea angling – once it has been removed from its shell, of course. These crabs can be found on rocky shorelines and under seaweed, and may also be obtained from commercial netsmen's fishing boats.

THE POPPER

This shows an effective set-up for black bass and pike, using a floating popper lure, to which is attached a lightly weighted worming dropper. The lure is best fished by being gently twitched and then allowed to float undisturbed for a time.

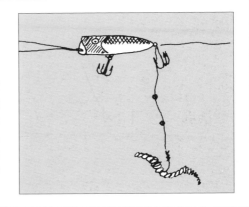

4. FISHING WITH LURES

SPINNER AND LIVE-BAIT

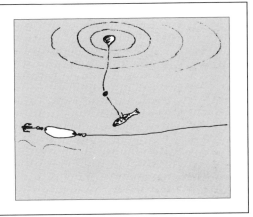

If you are fishing with a live-bait, it can be interesting to cast a spinning or wobbling lure close to it. One bait may serve as an attractor, while the other may be taken by the fish it attracts.

A MODIFIED POPPER

If a popper does not ride high enough in the water, this may be cured by drilling one or two holes in it. These should be sealed with a smear of epoxy glue.

AN IMPROVISED SPINNING LURE

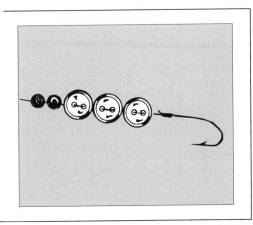

If you should find yourself in need of a spinning lure, a crude but effective one can be put together using two or three pale-coloured shirt buttons.

FLOATING LURE TACTIC

A floating/diving lure can also be used deeper in the water, when rigged up as shown here. A dropper of brass wire allows a weight to rest on the bottom, while the buoyancy of the lure keeps it fishing a little higher.

A HOOKLESS SPINNER

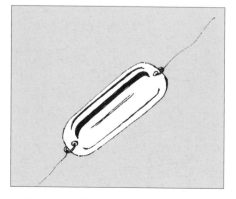

Sometimes good use is made of an extra attractor spinner, or 'dodger', which has no hook and is placed on the line above the terminal lure, to act as an eye-catching attractor to fish.

TANDEM SPINNER

A rig that has two revolving Mepps-type blades, often of different colours or patterns, can be useful in fast-flowing water, or to add weight for longer casting. It also presents more resistance to the water than a single blade.

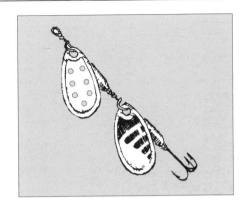

Have you ever used a lure with one revolving blade in tandem with a wobbling body? The results can be surprisingly good, especially when pike or black bass are the quarry. It is often best to use a darkish revolving blade with a bright, reflective wobbling lure body.

AN EASY-TO-MAKE SPINNER

It is easy to make a simple spinner of the type shown here. The basic shape can be cut with snips from a sheet of tin or other thin metal, with a swivel inserted into a hole drilled in the front and a treble hook attached at the rear, trailing from the middle of the tail. The body can be painted to your chosen pattern, and a weight should be added, perhaps painted as an eye. The tail fins should be twisted in opposite directions to provide a spinning movement.

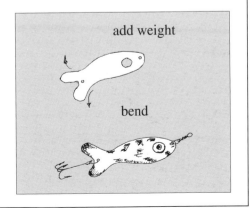

add weight

bend

COMBINATION LURE

Bizarre though it looks, this is a very deadly surface lure, consisting of a buoyant 'attractor' float and a hooked lure fished slightly subsurface. The surface wake of the floating part will draw the attention of a fish, which will then take the lower lure with its attractive streamers of brightly-coloured rubber or similar synthetics.

POPPERS

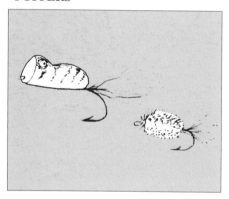

Popper lures have bodies of the largest possible size consistent with the buoyancy they must have to work properly. Balsa wood and various synthetics with low mass have been used, and one of the most widely used materials is deer-hair, which is relatively stiff, bulky and has hollow fibres containing air.

GOOD AND BAD POPPERS

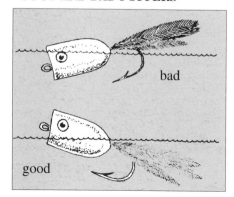

The popper is deservedly popular on account of its deadliness as a surface lure. On those occasions when it does not bring results, the reason may be poor balance and attitude in the water. A correctly balanced popper should float with a definite nose-up attitude, as shown here.

HEAVYWEIGHT LURE

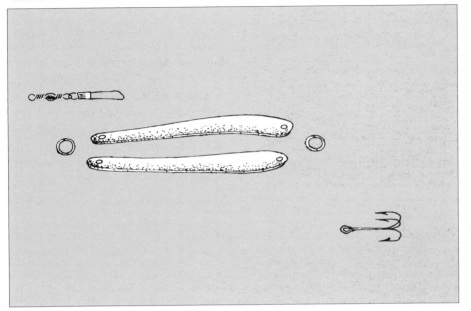

If a lure has to fish really deep, or has to be cast further than normal, the desired result can be achieved by mounting two identical lure bodies alongside one another, as shown here.

SINGLE-HOOKED LURE

There are times when a single hook on the end of a lure is preferable, such as when fishing close to the bottom, because of its reduced chances of snagging compared to a treble-hooked lure.

SPINNERS

If a lure with spinning blades, such as the celebrated Mepps, does not succeed in tempting fish, results may improve if it is exchanged for another with a darker or lighter blade colour, or by switching between flashing and matt-finished blades.

In late summer, and at times when water levels are low and clear, trout seem to be more readily taken on the smaller sizes of blade spinners, and those with subdued colours and less flashy finishes.

SNAGGING WITH LURES

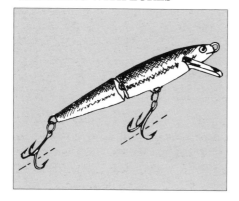

When the water being fished has a lot of underwater snags, the risks of a hook-up can be reduced by snipping off two of the three points of each treble hook, as shown here.

WORMING FOR BLACK BASS

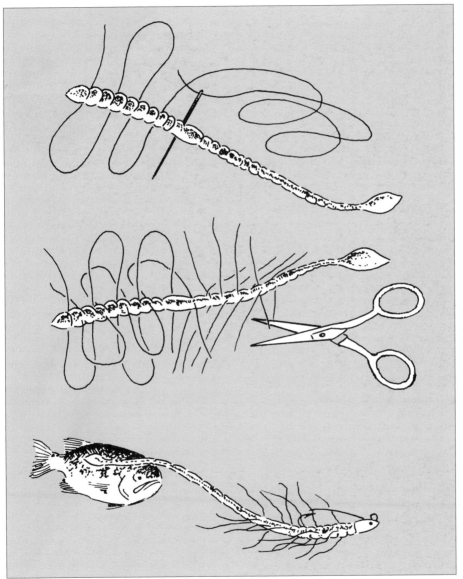

When fishing for black bass with a synthetic worm, the bait can be made considerably more attractive to the fish by garnishing it with sprouting lengths of monofilament. The illustration shows how this can be done by threading a length of line repeatedly through the artificial worm, leaving large loops which each produce two trailing threads when they are cut with scissors.

HOOKS THAT WON'T SNAG ON PLANTS

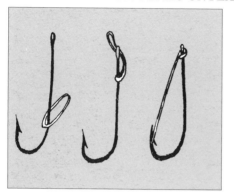

The top diagram shows an extremely simple way of setting up a hook so as to reduce its chances of becoming stuck in aquatic vegetation. A slender rubber band is threaded through the hook's eye, doubled over to secure it, and then hooked into the gape of the barb, thus forming an elastic guard over the hook.

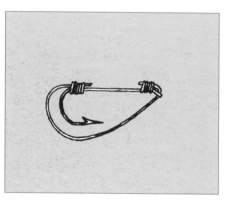

Another remedy for dealing with very weedy waters is to whip a loop of stiff heavyweight monofilament onto the hook, as shown in the lower diagram.

SMARTENING UP YOUR LURES

Lures that have been scratched or dulled can be smartened up or given an entirely new pattern or coloration by applying paints from the vast range available in hobby shops. Even waterproof synthetic paints are best given some additional protection by finishing them off with a coat of heavy-duty clear varnish.

A PIERCED LURE

A large lure need not be especially heavy if it is pierced with a network of holes of about 5 mm (0.2 in) in diameter. This piercing can also create additional turbulence which adds to the lure's erratic movement, making it even more attractive to fish.

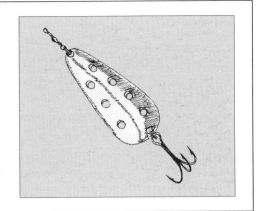

COLOUR VARIETY

Coloured beads can easily be added to the head of streamer-type flies and lures, and can be changed quickly during the day if required. A selection of beads of various colours can be conveniently kept on a safety-pin, as illustrated.

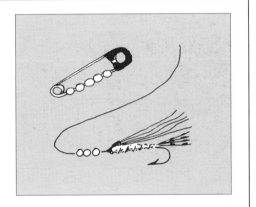

EYES FOR ATTACHING HOOKS

It often happens that a lure's hooks need to be replaced several times during the life of the main lure body. This is much more easily done if the hooks can be taken off and replaced on a split ring, rather than a fixed or screw-in eye.

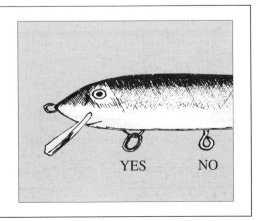

YES   NO

WORM-LURE JIG

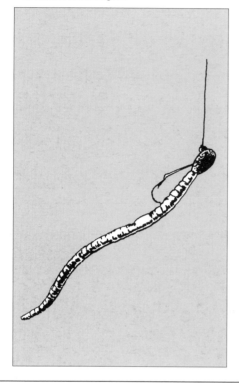

This jig deserves to be more widely known and used. It consists of a hook with a small weight pinched on just behind the eye. It can be used with many types of bait, including a synthetic worm, as shown here. It works well when fished with a gentle sink-and-draw action.

CHANGING HOOKS ON LURES

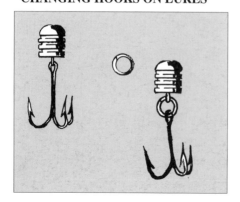

With a great many lures on the market, changing the treble hook can be very difficult. This can be over-come by a simple modification, in which a small split ring is used to link the hook with the eye at the base of the lure.

ANTI-SNAG WIRE FOR WEEDY WATERS

This diagram shows a good tip for when a spinning lure is to be used in weedy conditions. A length of fine, springy steel or brass wire should be wound firmly onto the central barrel or body of the swivel, with the ends allowed to stick out as shown. This helps to allow the lure to brush through weeds without getting caught.

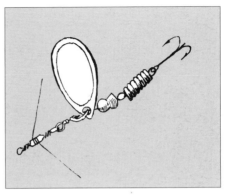

SWIVELS

A swivel is only really necessary when the action of the lure will otherwise cause a twisting of the line, and it will work best if it is best placed about 10–15 cm (4–6 in) above the lure.

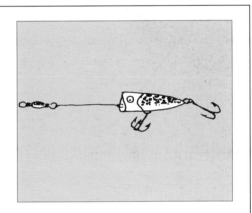

USING AN IMITATION FISH LURE

When fishing with a diving lure that is an imitation of a fish, do not retrieve line at a steady rate. Pause occasionally to allow the diving lure to pop up to the surface again, and then wind in some more to cause it to dive again. For trout, small pike and black bass it is best if the lure dives and surfaces at intervals of about 38.1–45.7 cm (15–18 in).

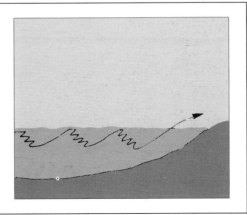

A SIMPLE SPINNING LURE

Early in the season a spinning lure often works best quite close to the bottom. To reduce the likelihood of getting snagged between rocks or hooked up on stones, replace the original treble hook with a single hook. This will not significantly reduce your ability to hook a fish.

WORKING A LURE

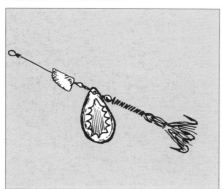

Sometimes a fish will be inclined to attack a quickly-retrieved, fast-spinning lure, and at other times a slower and more gentle movement will be preferable. It is therefore best to keep varying your speed of retrieve.

CASTING WITH A FIXED-SPOOL REEL

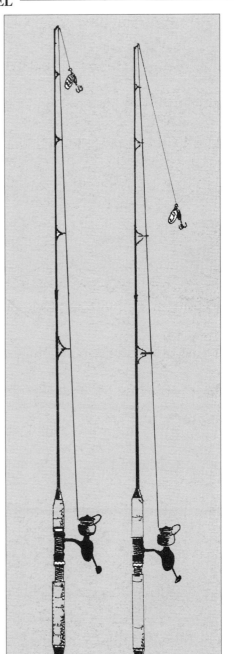

For good casting of a 3–6 g (0.1–0.2 oz) lure with a suitable monofilament line, a rod of about 1.8–2 m (6–6½ ft) long is best. Good timing, practice and familarity with your tackle are better than brute force when casting.

Select your weight and size of lure according to the distance and depth at which you reckon the fish to be lying. For short-distance, highly accurate casting with a rod and fixed-spool reel, begin with the lure dangling only a few inches outside the top ring. For maximum distance, however, begin with a heavier lure dangling up to 30.5–45.7 cm (12–18 in) from the tip.

FISHING WITH A POPPER

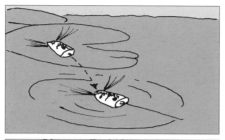

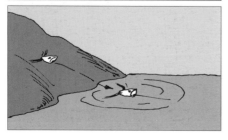

Poppers are fine lures for various fish species, including black bass. They produce the best results when the angler uses a wide repertoire of tactics and methods of presentation, depending upon circumstances, so that the lure appears as natural and enticing as possible.

Where fish are lying in the vicinity of roots, under overhanging growth and among aquatic vegetation, the popper can be presented nicely if it is cast so that it lands on a log or leaf, or on the water's edge before dropping onto the water. The risk of getting hung up is reduced if a non-snagging type of hook is used.

Black bass can be moody and unpredictable fish, so it pays to use a variety of presentational styles and line retrieval speeds, until you hit on the one that succeeds. Similar versatility also gives good results when fly-fishing for trout. Above all, be flexible and experimental in your tactics.

SPINNER AND WORM

This diagram shows a tackle set-up using a hookless spinning blade on the line above a worm fished on a single hook, and it can be especially effective when used in deep still-water conditions. The flickering blade acts as a good vibrational and visual attractor. Keep an eye on the worm, and change it as soon as it begins to look feeble or unnatural.

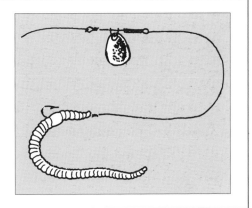

AN IMPROVISED SPINNING LURE

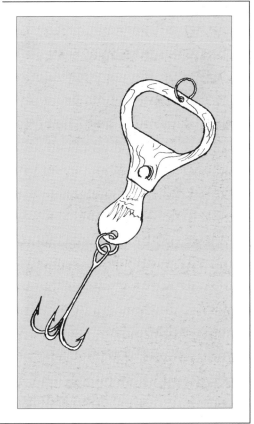

In addition to the many proprietary designs of lure available in tackle shops, less conventional but equally effective ones can be made at home. Here, the metal ring-pull from a drinks can has been drilled to take two split rings, one for the line and the other for a small treble hook, to make a cheap and simple little lure. Its action in the water can be highly attractive when the lure body is bent so as to impart a wobbling, flickering movement.

FREEING A SNAGGED LURE

Here is a simple, cheap and useful device for recovering lures that have become hooked up on underwater logs and similar snags. It involves a weight of around 100–150 g (3.5–5.3 oz), pierced with a metal wire that is formed into a 2.5-cm (1-in) spiral at the bottom, and with a top loop or eyelet to take a strong retrieval line or cord.

Run the fishing line into the spiral and lower the weight until it reaches the snagged lure. Its weight, and the strength of the retrieval line, make it possible to recover all but the most impossibly stuck lures.

AN ANTI-SNAG DEVICE

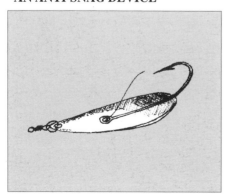

We often have to fish in places where there is plenty of submerged and emerging aquatic vegetation, and where there are major risks of getting snagged. This diagram shows the 'Silver Johnson' lure design, which can be bought in tackle shops or made at home. The chances of snagging are considerably reduced by the fine length of spring wire that lies in front of the hook and protects it.

5. FLY-FISHING

THREADING A FLY LINE

It is maddening to thread a fly line through the rod rings, only to have it all slide back down again and land at your feet! To prevent this, double the line over and thread it through as illustrated. That way, even if you let go of the line, the loop will spring open and prevent the line slipping back down.

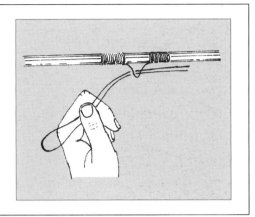

THE FLY'S DEPTH

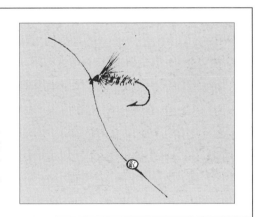

When using a wet fly or nymph, its position on the line and the depth at which it fishes can be adjusted by pinching a small single shot onto the line, to act as a stop.

DRYING OUT FLIES

When damp flies are taken off the leader, rusting will occur if you put them straight back into a fly box without drying them. Carry a small plastic bottle containing some hygroscopic material such as silica gel. Drop the damp fly in, and remove it later when it is thoroughly dry. You can make up a drying bottle yourself, or buy various types in tackle shops.

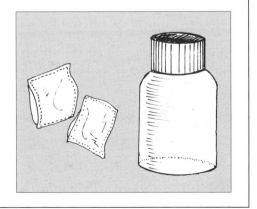

CHOOSING A FLY

Choosing which dry fly pattern to use is a major decision. Principles to bear in mind include similarity to the naturals that feeding fish are taking; balance and attitude when floating on the surface; and being clearly visible to the fish.

ATTACHING A FLY – 1

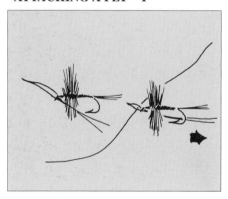

Especially in the dusk, it can be very difficult to tie a small fly onto a fine leader. Matters are made a lot easier if a number of flies are prepared in advance, with a short length of very fine monofilament looped through the eye, as shown. Then, threading the leader is greatly simplified by passing it through the loop and pulling it back through the eye.

ATTACHING A FLY – 2

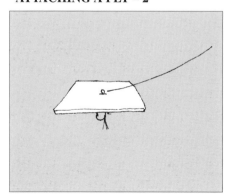

Here is a simple aid to assist with fly attachment. Carry a rectangular piece of white plastic with a slit cut in it. Push the fly into the slit, so that hackle hairs and other parts of the dressing are held back and clear of the protruding eye. Even in poor light, the eye and the leader should show up clearly against the white surface, to assist quick and accurate threading and knotting.

JOINING FLY LINE AND LEADER

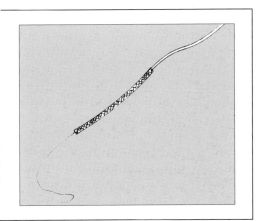

A braided section between the main fly line and the leader is an increasingly popular and highly effective way of securing them. It also helps to achieve a gradually tapering profile.

A FLUORESCENT LEADER

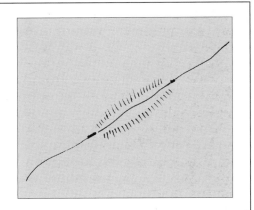

As a bite indicator, it can be useful to incorporate a short fluorescent section where the leader joins the main fly line. This shows up well in all but the poorest light, and helps in detecting very gentle takes.

GRIPPING THE FLY ROD

The grip you adopt may have to be altered, depending on whether you need to make a long, powerful cast, or a short and highly accurate one. Experiment to see which grip styles best suit you. The thumb-on-top grip (top) usually helps to achieve the best power and distance, while you may find that accuracy is better when the index finger is placed on top of the grip (bottom).

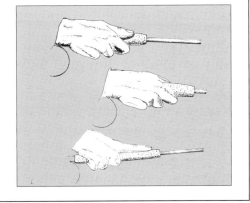

WHEN A FLY IS REFUSED

If fish come to a fly but turn away, something is clearly not right. The pattern is evidently attractive from a distance, but something puts the fish off at the last moment. Try using a smaller version of the same pattern, or a slightly lighter or darker variant of it.

FLY LINE CONNECTOR

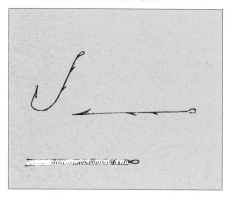

A fine bait hook with barbs on the shank can be straightened out and pushed into the core of the fly line to give a securely fixed eye on the end. A stainless steel hook is best, if eventual weakness through rusting is not to be a problem.

PRESERVING FLY LINE QUALITY

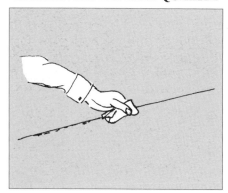

To keep a fly line in good condition, it should occasionally be thoroughly washed and wiped down, and then a good quality line conditioner should be applied with a soft cloth. This will maintain suppleness, prevent cracking and extend the line's life. Excess conditioner should be wiped off before the line is used again.

BLACK BASS ON A FLY

June and July are perhaps the best months for taking black bass on a fly. A pattern with a buoyant deer-hair body, winged and tailed as shown, can be very productive, especially when fishing from a boat and casting alongside marginal vegetation.

TO RISE A TROUT

If you are casting over trout and presenting your fly well, yet failing to get a take, it is best to keep changing your fly until a successful pattern or size brings a result. If you feel that the fly dressing and colour are right, it is best to go first for smaller versions and then, if the fish still do not respond, to increase the fly's size progressively.

FISHING DOWNSTREAM

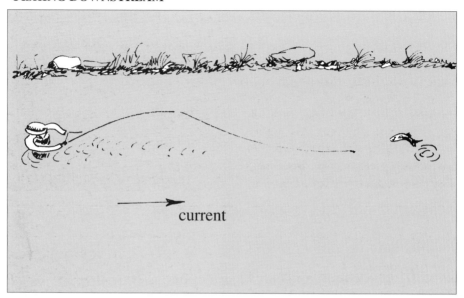

current

The orthodox way to fish a dry fly on a river is to cast it upstream. However, (provided fishery regulations allow it) surprisingly good results can come from allowing a dry fly to float with the current downstream of you, especially if you can manoeuvre it towards a steadily-feeding fish.

CASTING CORRECTLY

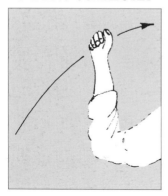

Some of the most common problems with fly-casting stem from incorrect use of the wrist. A strong, well timed and accurate cast is achieved by keeping the wrist locked, and not allowing the lower arm and rod angle to go too far past the vertical. The correct movement can be practised by using an upright surface such as a wall or the edge of a door to stop the arm coming too far back.

FLUORESCENT BITE INDICATOR

When nymphing, the detection of very gentle takes is made much easier if there is a fluorescent marker on the leader, which may consist either of a section of dayglo line (as shown here) or a small high-visibility floating bob on the leader.

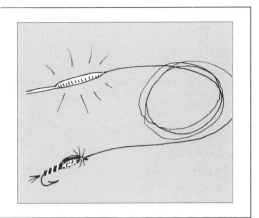

FLY BOX

Self-adhesive strips of synthetic foam, of the type used for sealing windows against draughts, can be used to make a first-class fly box. They should be laid in rows inside a simple box, as shown, and the flies can then be hooked into them. This allows flies to be laid out clearly, and prevents crushing of hackles, tangling or other problems.

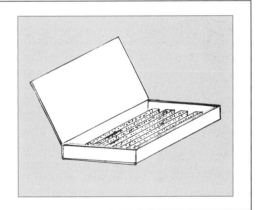

FLY SIZES

There is an old rule of thumb that the larger fly sizes are appropriate for the early season, and in autumn, with the small sizes best in summer. While this is a good rule to follow, always have a selection of sizes for a particular pattern, so that you can ring the changes and offer what the fish will take most readily.

DIFFERING RISE FORMS

If a fly-fisher is alert and can identify the different ways in which trout take their natural food, it will give important clues to the flies and tactics that are most likely to be productive.

As the diagrams show, a bulging rise may mean that the fish are feeding on nymphs and ascending invertebrates just below the surface, while tailing rises tend to indicate the fish are pouncing down onto food lower in the water.

The selection of suitable patterns, and the depth at which flies should be fished, can therefore be deduced from watching the feeding fish. Once a fish has been caught, an examination of its stomach contents will provide important evidence of what they are eating and how it can best be imitated.

DIFFERING RISE FORMS (Continued)

Figure 4 shows the typical way in which trout will take emerging duns and spinners on the surface. A leaping rise, as shown in Figure 5, may characterise fish that are taking insects just as they rise off the surface, while Figure 6 shows the slight bulge or hump in the water's surface created by a fish taking ascending nymphs.

PALMER DRESSING

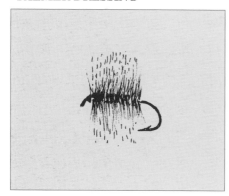

If you are fishing with a dry fly towards dusk and in deteriorating light conditions, it is much easier to keep an eye on your fly if a pale pattern dressed palmer-fashion is used. The palmer hackle gives buoyancy and high visibility, qualities that are also useful in fast, broken water.

CHANGING A FLY LINE

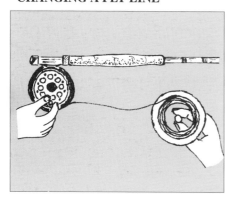

When winding a new or replacement fly line onto a reel, it is important to do it in such a way that the line comes steadily off its spool or hank under uniform tension, without any twists that could give rise to line kinking and impede free running of the line.

TROUT IN FAST WATER

A dry fly can often be more easily fished in rapid water than in calm spots. The fly's rapid movement in tumbling water will disguise any unnatural twitches or vibrations that would be highly visible on the surface of calm water. Fish feeding in fast water also have very little time to study potential food items before attacking them.

TYING ON SMALL FLIES

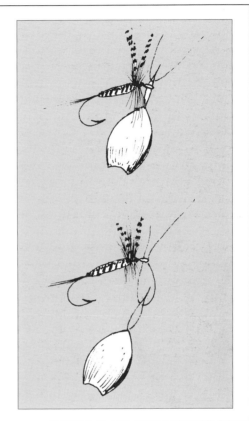

If threading the leader tippet on small flies presents a problem, try using a needle-threading tool, as used by seamstresses. The fine, stiff point is easily put through the eye of even a small hook, then springs open to give an elongated loop through which the tippet can be threaded, before it is pulled back through the eye of the hook. This tool is also useful when preparing to tie any knot that requires the leader line to be looped twice through the eye.

FLY RETRIEVER

Who has not, at some point, managed to hook up a fly on an overhanging tree or bush? A retriever hook and cord, as shown here, can usually solve the problem. The straight leg (marked A) is inserted in the top ring of the fly rod, and the triangular hook can then be placed over the offending branch or twig and pulled down by means of the attached line.

LINE MARKINGS

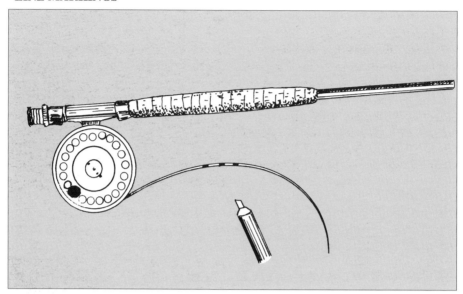

Markings on the fly line, made with waterproof ink, are extremely helpful in indicating how much line has been run off the reel. Every fly rod works best when an optimal amount of line is run out and aerialised. Further marks can be applied as desired, for example to indicate when the end of the level section of a double-taper line has been reached.

AN INSECT NET

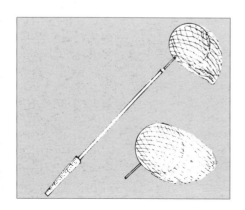

An insect-collecting net, easily made at home, is useful when fish are seen to be feeding on hatching ephemerids. By catching some examples and examining them closely, matching the hatch with an artificial fly can be done with more confidence. A pensioned-off telescopic fly rod, with its rings removed, makes an excellent handle; and a fixed length of aluminium tubing of 3–4 mm (0.12–0.16 in) diameter is also a handy and light shaft

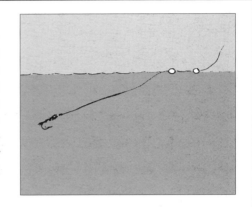

BITE INDICATOR

When fishing with a nymph or well-sunk wet fly, very gentle takes can easily go unnoticed. A small slip-on oval of polystyrene placed towards the top of the leader acts as a very useful and clearly visible bite indicator, and it can be worth using two of them when the light is poor, or when using some form of natural bait.

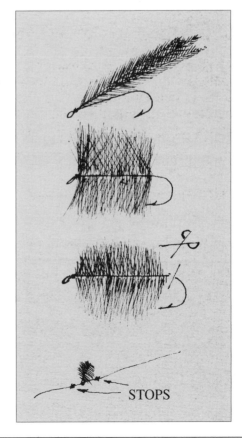

One of the essential challenges in fishing upstream with a nymph is in knowing exactly when a fish takes. Various devices and gadgets have been developed to help, including brightly-coloured floating bite indicators and suchlike. This diagram shows another useful method, which involves using a body of spun deer-hair or other highly buoyant material on the shank of a hook that has been cut off above the bend. This can be attached directly to the line, or allowed to move between an upper and lower stop, made either with knots or small split shot.

STOPS

DRY FLY BITE INDICATOR

A dry fly can be fished in conjunction with a nymph, and vice versa, in such a way that both flies are presented to the fish. If the floating fly is taken, the angler will clearly see it; and if the nymph is taken, the dry fly acts as a handy bite indicator.

If the nymph is the principal fly, especially in fast or broken water, it is wise to use a dry fly with a palmered or spun deer-hair body, which will have a particularly buoyant, high-floating and conspicuous appearance.

SAMPLING NET

To catch and examine samples of the surface insects and subsurface nymphs that are being carried along in the current, a simple and effective sampling net can be made from a piece of very fine-meshed material about 0.6 m (2 ft) long and 45.7 cm (18 in) deep. With a rod or stick handle at each end, this can be submerged and held in the water, and the whole device rolls up neatly when it is no longer required.

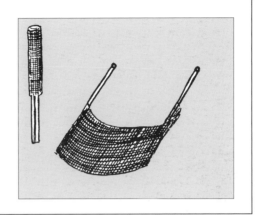

FLY FLOATANT

It is not difficult to make your own waterproof floatant. Ten grams (0.4 ounces) of white paraffin wax flakes should be melted in 50 grams (1.8 ounces) of carbon tetrachloride, in a container placed in hot water, and the liquid poured into a small container.

TANDEM FLIES

When fly-fishing for trout, a pair of flies fished in tandem may produce results when other approaches have failed. Tandem flies may be similarly dressed or have contrasting patterns, but it is always best to have them the same size.

INSECT NET

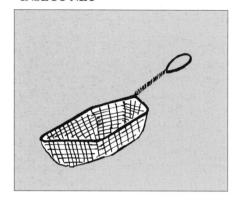

Have you ever wanted to examine a particular fly that was being carried along by the river? It is difficult to do so without some means of capturing some samples. This can be done with a small, light, wire-framed net of the kind shown here, which can be compact enough to fit into a pocket of your fishing jacket.

HOOK POINTS

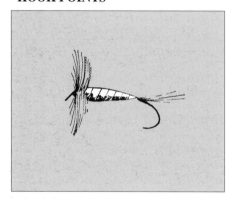

In both dry and wet fly-fishing, it is extremely common for hooks points to become damaged or blunted, which may make hooking a fish almost impossible. If a fly is fished continuously over a long period such damage becomes almost inevitable, so it is important to check on the condition of hook points regularly during a long fishing session.

FLY CONTAINER

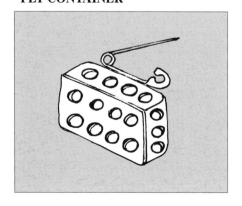

A small plastic box of 3.8–5.1 cm (1½–2 in), pierced with ventilation holes and fastened to your fishing coat with a safety-pin, makes a good storage and drying container for the flies you have used in the course of a day's fishing. Later, they can be removed, dried and returned to your main fly boxes.

A FLY HOOK FOR NATURALS

Here is a diagram of the special hook used for fly-fishing (especially dapping) using the natural insect. On the hook shank is a spring-clip for holding the insect, which is a traditional method of mounting a natural mayfly for still-water fishing.

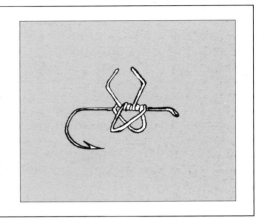

FINDING THE LINE TIP

Nothing is more annoying than to have the end of a line disappear among the many coils on the reel. A great many reels have some means of securing the line end, such as by looping or tying it through a hole in the spool. If a reel does not have such a hole or other place for looping the end of the line, it is a simple matter to drill a suitable hole.

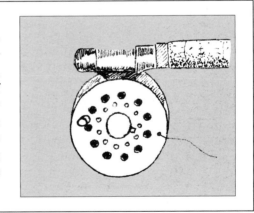

LINE DISPENSER

It is easy to make a cheap and handy line dispenser for leaders and tippets, using a plastic 35 mm camera film container and a few plastic bottle tops. The tops can be glued together in pairs, as shown, to make little spools, and when loaded with lengths of monofilament of different test strengths, these can be stacked inside the camera film container. Line of the desired strength can then be drawn out of the appropriately marked hole.

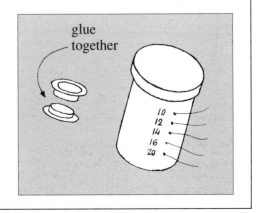

glue together

10
12
14
16
20

NYMPHS

Small nymphs are best used in clear and fast-flowing waters, while the larger sizes on size 6 and 8 hooks give best results when fished deep in slow moving or still waters. Weighted nymphs also have their uses in both types of conditions.

LIGHTLY-DRESSED FLIES

Very lightly-dressed flies with a simple body will fish with a very pleasing and attractive action if the hackle is mounted so that the individual fibres point slightly forwards. This causes them to flex in the current, simulating the movements of a natural insect.

CLEARING HOOK EYES

The fine point of a needle is a good way of ensuring that a hook eye is clear of any dried varnish or other obstruction. It is well worth checking all your flies like this at home, rather than have a problem fly to contend with by the waterside.

SEDGE FLY (TRICHOPTERA) LARVAE

Every fly-fisher will be familiar with the general appearance of the cased larvae of the various sedge flies, but it is interesting to be able to identify the principal species of sedges from the distinctive appearance of their larval cases. It is often easier to identify the cases than the swimming nymphs or the emerging insects.

The illustrated cased larvae are from the top downwards:

- *Limnephalus lunatus* is the cinnamon sedge, whose case is composed of fragments of vegetation, and typically measures about 2 cm (0.8 in) long and 4 mm (0.16 in) in diameter.
- *Pothamophylax latipennis* is the large cinnamon sedge, with a case constructed of grains of sand.
- The brown sedge *Anabolia nervosa* has a case made of particles of gravel interwoven with long fibres and twigs, which prevent it from being too easy a mouthful for predators.
- *Halesius radiatus* is the well-known caperer, and its case is somewhat similar to that of the brown sedge, but composed of rather larger grit particles.
- The case of the grannom *Brachycentrus subnubilis* cannot be mistaken for any of the others because of its square-sectioned shape.
- The silver or grey sedge *Odontocerum albicorne* has a distinctive larval case, rather conical and curved in shape, while the case of the medium sedge *Goera pilosa* is about 5 mm (0.2 in) in diameter and 1.5 cm (0.6 in) long.

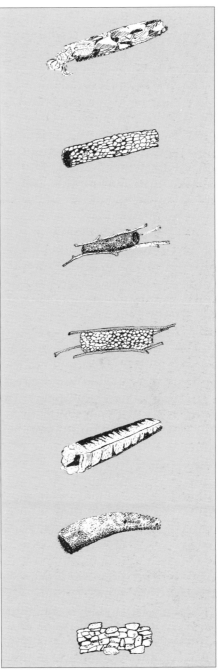

6. FLY-TYING

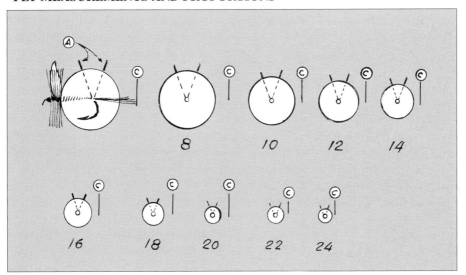

One of the most common errors in fly-tying is to end up with a lack of proportion between the various elements that comprise the pattern and dressing. This diagram may be helpful in avoiding this problem, and it shows the relationship of hook size to hackle and tail lengths.

PORTABLE VICE

A simple and effective portable vice that allows flies to be tied by the water's edge can be made at home quite readily, as shown here, by modifying a pair of finely pointed pliers so they can be clamped firmly shut.

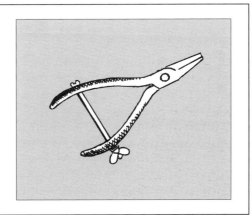

FLY-TYING BASE BOARD

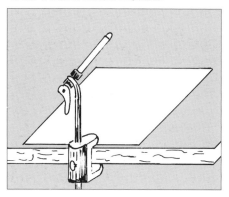

It is best to tie flies in conditions of good light and clear contrast. This is easily achieved by ensuring that your vice is placed so that you are looking at the fly against a very pale or pure white matt background.

FLIES FOR BLACK BASS

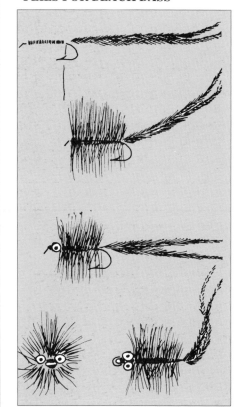

An extremely good black bass fly is the serpent or snake pattern shown here. It is tied on a large hook, and can be of whatever colour takes your fancy, although mixtures of black and white are widely favoured. Bright and prominent eyes are followed by a bushily palmered body, with two trailing streamers of peacock herl.

GLUE PENS

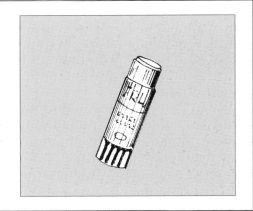

Tying thread can be quickly and easily prepared by drawing it over a glue stick or similar office adhesive. Treated like this, it readily accepts and holds dubbing.

HACKLE LENGTHS

Here is another way of making sure that the length of the hackle will be appropriate for the hook size. Having pierced the central point of this diagram with a dubbing needle, the feather can be held against it. The intersection of the various lines will show the length of hackle that is appropriate for a particular hook size.

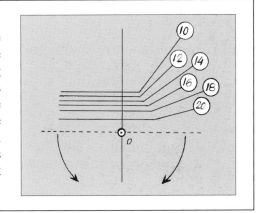

HOOK PROTECTION

Never risk damaging your hook points by clamping them in the jaws of the tying vice. When it is time to varnish the head of the finished fly, pass a length of monofilament through the eye of the hook, to prevent it becoming blocked up with the varnish.

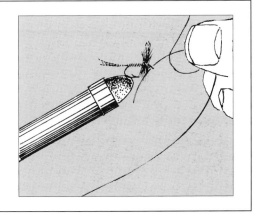

'BUGS'

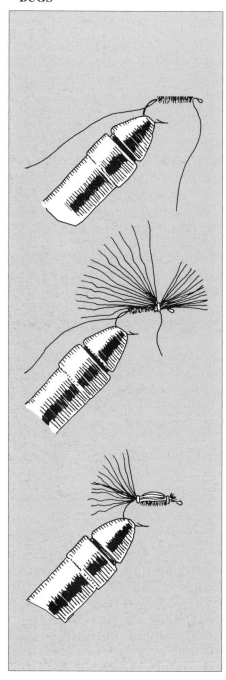

Once considered rather unorthodox, bug patterns are now widely and very successfully used for trout. The construction of a bug dressing is very straightforward, and begins with building up a body on the hook's shank (sizes 12 to 16 are best) using two or three strands of peacock herl. A pinch of deer-hair is tied in at the head and drawn back over the upper part of the body, to be tied off just before the beginning of the bend. This smooth body covering simulates an insect's wing cases, and the end of the deer-hair fibres trail to form a tail.

'BUGS' (Continued)

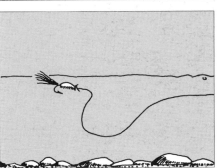

A bug can be fished on the surface like a dry fly (top) but when retrieved against the current it gives the impression of an insect that is struggling against the flow. When fished on a sinking leader, its buoyancy causes it to rise and simulate the upward movement of a rising, emergent ephemerid. Alternatively, it may be fished deeper in the water, in the manner of a nymph. Thus, without changing the fly, this versatile pattern can be deployed in a variety of ways, and it deserves to be even more widely used than it is.

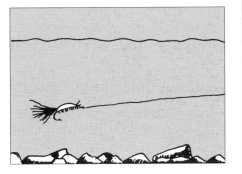

THE POPPER

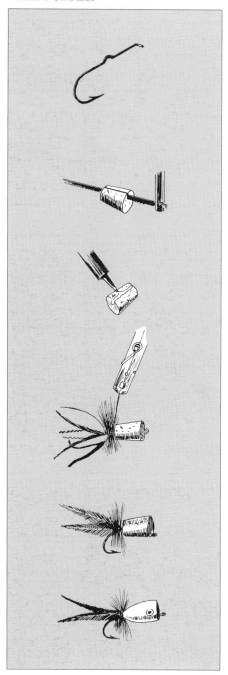

Making excellent poppers is easy, requiring no special materials apart from the hook with its distinctive hump in the shank, which prevent the body rotating on the shank. But if you cannot obtain these, it is still possible to use a conventional hook for this lure.

Use a fine-toothed, thin-bladed saw to make a slit about 5 mm (0.2 in) deep in the pre-shaped cork body, and once the hook shank has been placed in this, seal everything permanently in position with an epoxy-type glue. Now the basic popper is complete, and the rest of the work involves decorating and trimming it into final form. If you don't have a fly-tying vice, a small Mole clamp wrench or locking pliers will do.

Long, fine and flexible hackles are added by winding on a feather behind the cork body, at the end of the hook shank. (A clothes peg makes a perfectly adequate pair of hackle pliers.) The trailing tails can be made in various forms, bearing in mind that a heavily feathered tail may make the popper more difficult to cast. Paint and varnish the body to suit your fancy, add two artificial eyes, and the popper is complete.

A TYING VICE ACCESSORY

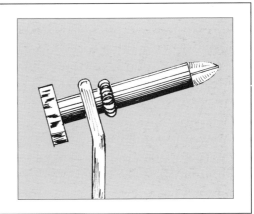

A little spring wound round and fastened to the vice arm, as shown, is invaluable for gripping tying thread and holding other little bits and pieces of dressing materials while you are at work on a fly.

DETACHED-BODY FLY

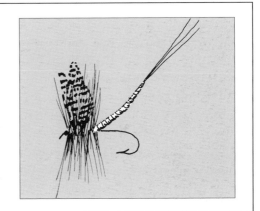

A 'detached body' is the term we use to denote a dressing in which the fly's body is largely free from the hook shank, apart from one forward anchoring point. This type of body is chiefly used when dressing representations of large ephemerids such as the mayflies.

QUILL BODY

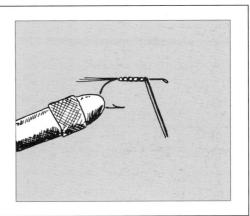

One of the best ways of making a fly body that has perfectly formed segments is to wind on a peacock quill.

FLY BODIES

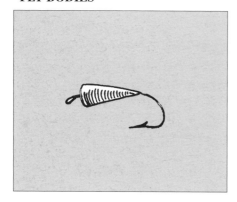

You can make fly bodies by mixing threads of fibreglass with epoxy adhesive, winding them around the hook shank, and moulding them to the outline you want. When dried and hardened, the result will be a virtually indestructible body made up of polyester layers.

WEIGHTED NYMPHS

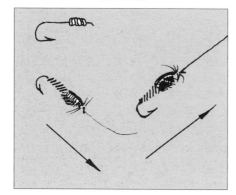

Weighted nymphs can have an attractive working movement if the weight is added by turns of fine lead wire wound on to the hook shank under the thorax area of the dressing. Nymphs weighted like this will fish with a sink-and-draw motion that is attractive to trout.

NYMPHS

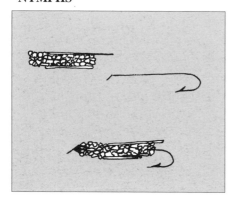

Excellent nymphs can be made from the larval cases of sedge flies (trichoptera). Use a long-shanked hook, and pack the inside with a mixture of glue and fine lead shavings. The head can be formed from turns of black silk, to give the final shape shown here.

THE 'HAIR-BUG'

The tying of hair-bug flies can be done in various ways, to produce finished lures that can be highly successful for many species of freshwater fish, including trout and black bass. The deer-hair of which they are made is naturally hollow, and the air within it gives it lightness and great buoyancy. Once in place, the spun hair can be clipped and trimmed to give a variety of finished shapes and profiles.

These flies are easier to make than it might appear from the diagrams. Once a pinch of hair has been tied in to form the tail, a succession of further pinches are wound onto the hook shank. The tightening of the lightly waxed tying silk causes it to spin and the individual fibres to stand erect and perpendicular to the axis of the hook shank. Here, the first bunch of hair is trimmed down to make a neat and streamlined rear body section, after which a tuft of fibres is tied in to create wings. The blunt-headed forward section of the body is completed by trimming back a further bunch of spun hair. The spun deer-hair provides the basis for a great deal of improvisation and variation, by adding colours, eyes etc.

DUBBING

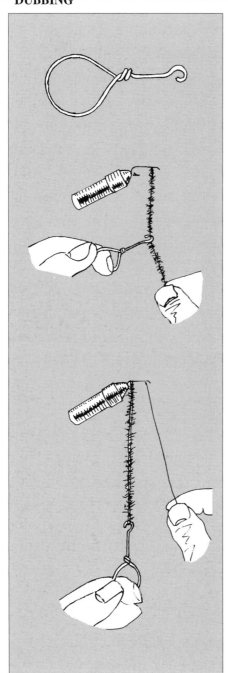

Dubbing is the fly-tier's method of applying small fibres of various materials to a section of waxed tying silk, so that they adhere and are twisted to form a fluffy rope of dressing. This can be wound around the shank of the hook to form a fly body.

A great many different types and colours of natural and synthetic fibres can be used in this way. The dubbed material can be wound over a weighted section, if the fly is intended to sink, or may incorporate buoyant synthetic fibres that will keep the fly afloat. Hackles and wings can be added as particular patterns and dressings call for them, but a dubbed body is the foundation of a great many of the most important and successful flies.

DUBBING (Continued)

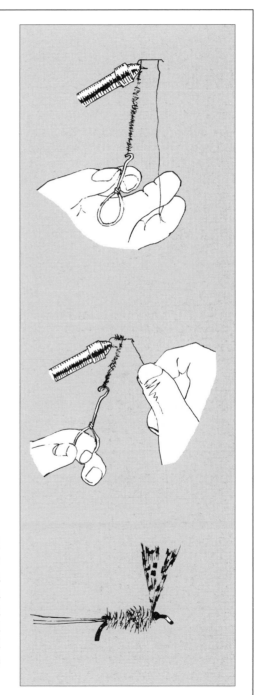

The diagrams show how a useful gadget can be made very simply, by twisting a length of wire to form a hooked tool. This helps to keep a dubbed section of silk separate from other elements and materials, and allows the dubbed silk to be wound on easily, accurately and under the correct amount of tension.

FLY-FISHING AT DUSK

When fishing a dry fly as the last of the light fades, it becomes much easier to see your fly if the dressing incorporates two or three contrasting colours. White, hot orange and dayglo yellow are particularly good.

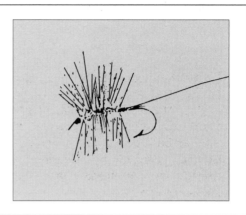

HACKLE PILERS

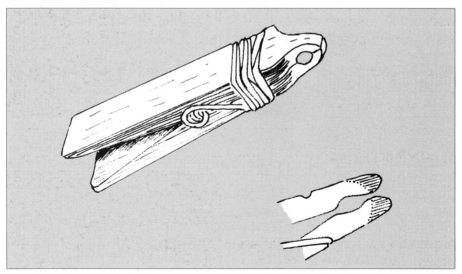

A useful pair of hackle pliers can be made quickly and cheaply from a clothes-peg. The jaws of the pliers need to be trimmed down to give a fine-nosed shape, and it is advisable to supplement the force of the wire spring by winding on a thin rubber band, as shown.

7. SEA FISHING

DISPOSABLE WEIGHTS

Old spark plugs cost nothing, and can be used as handy disposable weights. The plug's body has plenty of grooves around which a line or trace can be fastened, and a line can also be attached by slipping it through the electrode gap and tapping the gap shut.

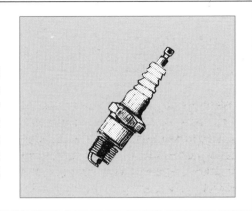

HOOK EYES

Sea fishing can involve putting very heavy pressures on fishing lines. If this force is transmitted to the eye of the hook, a poor quality one may pull out and open up under the strain. Many anglers therefore prefer to attach the line more directly to the shank of the hook, as shown.

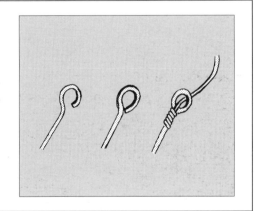

THE BUBBLE FLOAT

When using a bubble float for sea angling, do not attach the float directly to the main line. A length of strong monofilament, or stainless steel wire, can be attached to the float as shown, and the two loops used as attachment points.

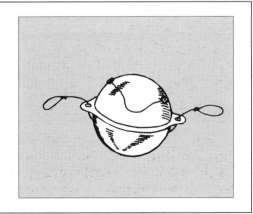

DEEP TROLLING

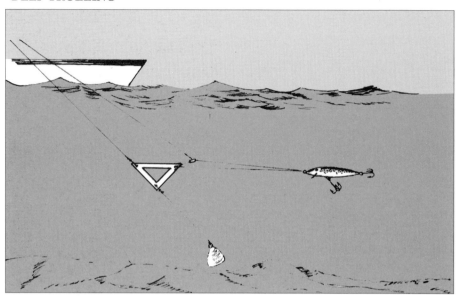

When deep trolling a lure or bait, the rig shown here is an excellent set-up to use. Note that the heavy trolling weight does not bear directly upon the lure, which is held well down in the water but still free to work with an attractive action. When a fish takes, the fishing line breaks free of the weight line, and allows the fish to be played directly, without the encumbrance of a heavy weight.

MULLET RIG

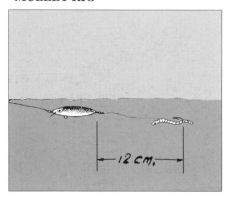

Shown here is one of the techniques used by mullet anglers, in which the conventional treble hook is removed from the tail of the lure, and replaced with a short further length of line with a single hook baited with a lugworm. A floating Rapala-type lure is best, and the results can be very pleasing.

LURE-FISHING WITH A WEIGHT

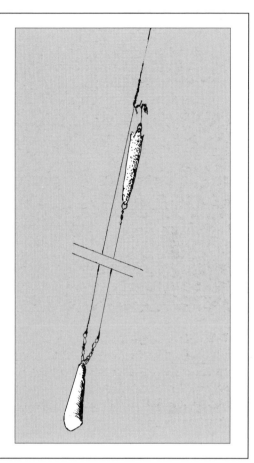

This diagram shows a suitable set-up for fishing with a weight and lure, for long-distance casting and working the lure deep in the water. When preparing to cast, the lure is doubled back up the line and held there by hooking one leg of the treble into another little hook placed on the trace. This prevents tangling, and means that the whole rig can be cast with the heavy weight hanging right at the end. Once the rig hits the water, the lure quickly disengages from the little hook and fishes freely at the end of the trace.

A MOULD FOR WEIGHTS

Heavy lead weights for sea fishing are not cheap, and a high proportion of them are lost. It therefore pays to make your own weights by melting scrap lead and using one of the many moulds that can be obtained from tackle suppliers. Alternatively, you can make your own moulds by taking plaster casts of the weights you wish to make.

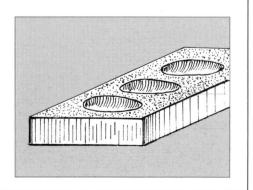

SHORELINE SEA FISH

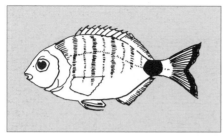

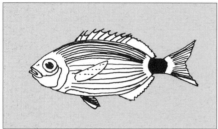

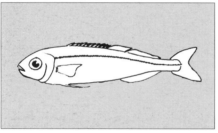

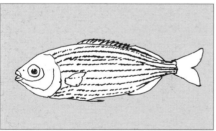

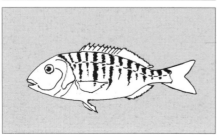

If you are a sea angler, the various species shown here will be familiar; and if you intend to take your rods with you on a seaside holiday, these are some of the fish that you may encounter:

Blacktail *Diplodus sargus* – there are three other species in this family, and typical weights are around 0.5 kg (1 lb).

Saddled bream *Oblada melanura* – although mainly a herbivore, this species will take worms and crustaceans.

Bogue *Boops boops* – found along the coasts in spring and autumn. Typical weight just under 0.2 kg (0.5 lb).

Saupe bream *Boops salpa* – found in large shoals along rocky coastlines.

Sea bream *Pagellus mormyrus* – often ventures into tidal inlets and estuaries.

SHORELINE SEA FISH (Continued)

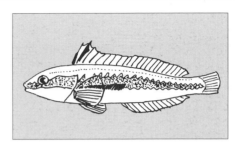

Rainbow wrasse *Coris julis* – a real riot of colours, this fish abounds deep down below rocky seashores.

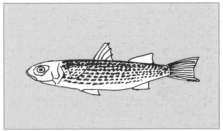

Mullet *Mugil cephalus* – there are 5 similar-looking species, and the flatheaded mullet can grow to as much as a metre (3.3 ft) long and a weight of 6.4 kg (14 lb).

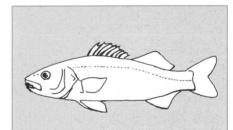

Sea bass *Morone labrax* – one of the most sought-after of sea fish, bass can grow to 11.3 kg (25 lb) and more.

Damselfish *Chromis chromis* – this species has an attractive blueish-black coloration, and is occasionally found in harbours.

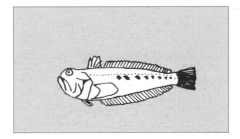

Greater and lesser weavers *Trachinus draco and T. vipera* – these are dangerous fish, and ought not to be touched. They have sharp, poisonous spines in their dorsal fins, and it will not brighten up your holiday if you are speared by them!

SURF-CASTING RIG

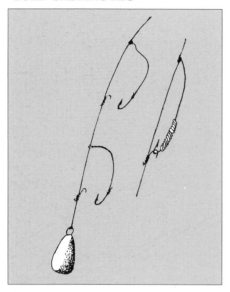

Powerful rods and heavy weights are necessary for successful surf-casting, and sometimes it can be nearly impossible to use delicate baits, which easily get flung off by the force of the cast. To overcome this, it is worth using a rig of the type shown here. If the baited hooks on the droppers are looped into place on the small retaining hooks, the baits do not flail about in the air during the cast. Once the rig lands in the water, the baited hooks quickly disengage and the baits should still be securely in place.

RIG SUGGESTION

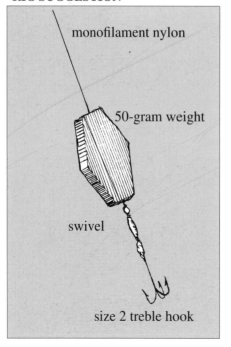

monofilament nylon

50-gram weight

swivel

size 2 treble hook

Sole, plaice and other flatfish can be caught using the set-up shown here, which involves a flat lead weight of 50–75 g (1.8–2.6 oz) and a treble hook size 2–4. The best places to fish are unfrequented beaches and at the mouths of estuaries. While this rig can be used with a rod and line, it is also possible to use it quite successfully on a hand line.

8. KNOTS

A KNOT FOR LACES

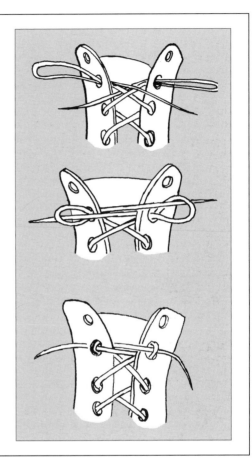

Nothing is more exasperating than laces that keep coming undone! It is always a nuisance, and can sometimes even be dangerous. The solution is simple, and is illustrated in this diagram. The ends of the lace are doubled over and passed through the eyelets as shown, so that they form two locking loops. These grip the lace and hold it firmly, even if the final knot comes undone. It may not even be necessary to make a further knot – just tuck the lace ends out of the way.

AN IMPROVED CLINCH KNOT

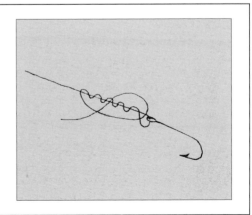

If you use a clinch-type knot to attach a fly or hook, it is wise to pass the free end of the line through the knot twice, as shown. This way, the knot tightens on the line and clinches it at two points.

KNOT FOR PLUG LURES

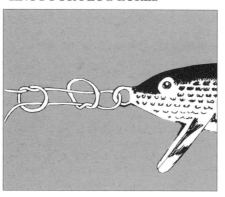

It is important that plugs and similar lures are fixed with a secure knot that also allows the lures to waggle and move as freely as possible, without too much twisting or kinking motion being transmitted to the line. The knots shown are recommended.

DROPPERS

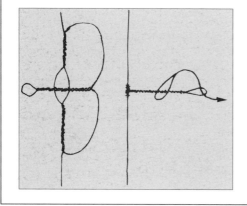

When fishing deep, with dropper-type offshoots from the main line, one of the best ways to avoid tangles is shown in the diagram. The loop system also makes it easy to change baits and hooks.

THE CLOVE HITCH

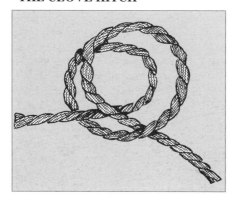

Do you know how to tie a clove hitch? It is simple to do, and is arguably the most useful of all knots onboard a boat. With a little practice, the clove hitch can be tied in an instant with a couple of twists of the wrist, to make a rope or line secure.

JOINING LINE TO REEL

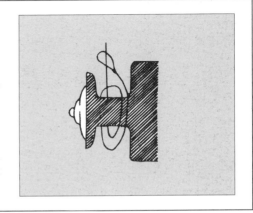

There are a great many methods for attaching a line to the spool of a reel. The one shown here is one of the simplest, neatest and most secure. Once the reel is turned to take in more line, this method of attachment will not slip.

A HOOK ON A WIRE

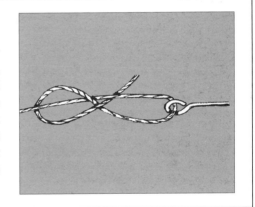

If you want to attach a hook directly to wire, and do not have gloves, pliers or other tools to twist and manipulate the wire, this is about the only possible knot you can use. It works even better if the wire consists of a number of smaller braided or twisted wires. The free end should be cut off short if possible.

THE NAIL KNOT

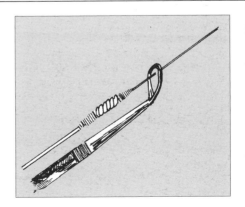

One of the recommended ways of joining a fly line to a butt or leader is by means of a nail knot. The basic knot can be improved if its coils are lightly varnished or smeared with epoxy. When correctly formed, this knot will slip through the tip ring easily and without snagging.

THE BIMINI TWIST

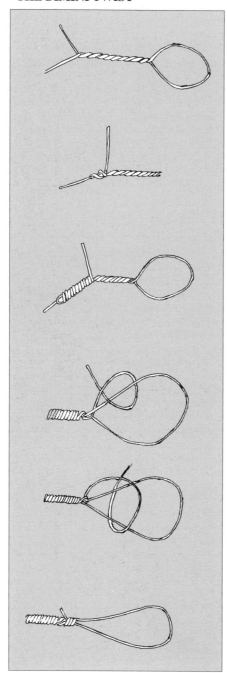

Do you know how to tie the bimini twist? It is almost *the* compulsory knot for sea angling, especially when fishing under the rules of the International Game Fishing Association (IGFA). It is without doubt the strongest knot to make a loop in the end of any type of line, and if the loop is big enough, it can be used to attach any kind of bait or lure. It also makes the changing of lures very simple. It is most easily made in Dacron lines, which are normally used for deep-sea fishing, but is also a good knot for all but the finest monofilament lines.

BAIT-MOUNTING HOOK

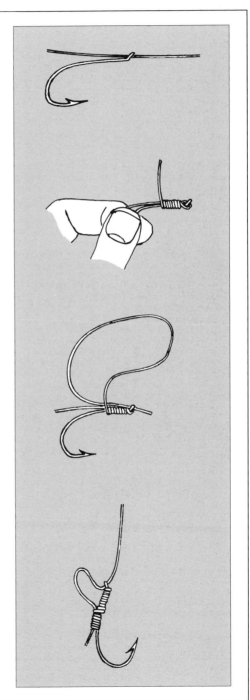

The hook set-up shown here is one of the best ways of attaching a natural bait to a hook. It is put together using a normal eyed hook and a length of monofilament that should not be too fine. The diagrams show how the knots and loop are constructed.

The monofilament is first passed through the hook's eye and drawn back to just beyond the bend. The other end is wound around the hook shank about 10–15 times, and a loop is then made, as shown in the third diagram. To the rear of the loop another 8 or 10 turns should be made, so that the tying finishes with a loop that can be enlarged or tightened by releasing or pulling the line.

The loop above the well-whipped shank of the hook can be used to attach almost any type of natural bait, including a bunch of worms or strips of sardine.

IMPROVING KNOTS

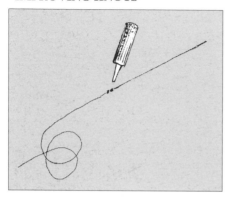

Knots in a line or leader can be made even more secure and smooth-running, especially in a very light line, if a small drop of superglue is smeared over the finished knot and allowed to dry thoroughly before use.

THE CLINCH KNOT

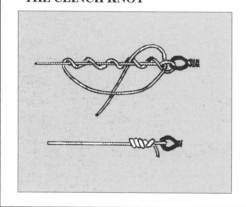

The clinch knot is a quick, simple and strong method of attaching any hook, swivel or other eyed connector to your line, and retains about 80 per cent of the line's strength. A useful tip is to moisten the coils of monofilament before pulling the knot tight.

TIGHTENING KNOTS

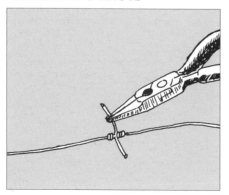

When finishing off knots in monofilament line of more than about 7.3–9 kg (16–20 lb) breaking strain it is wise to use a small pair of pincers or pliers to pull the knot tight. This makes a much better job than it is possible to achieve by using one's fingers alone.

THE PALOMAR KNOT

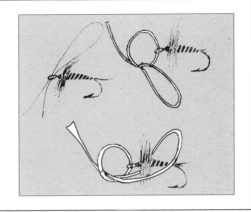

The Palomar knot is often used by sea anglers, and is also a most useful knot when fly-fishing with a very fine tippet. With tiny flies, the main difficulty is passing the line twice through the eye of the hook.

THE BLOOD-KNOT

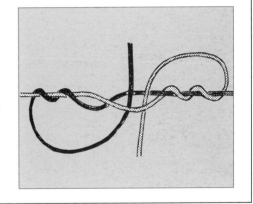

The blood-knot is perhaps the best means of joining two lines of equal or nearly equal thickness. It does not slip, and retains about 80 per cent of the strength of the line. It is not suitable for joining two lines which are of significantly different diameters.

9. TACKLE PREPARATION AND CARE

ROD RINGS

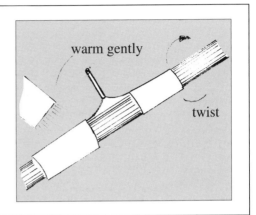

One of the best ways to give your rod rings a professional and well finished appearance is to use sleeves of PVC which shrink when they are heated. Rotate the rod in the air flow from a hair-drier.

TIP FOR WHIP-FINISHING

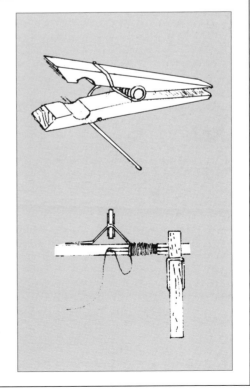

A household clothes-peg can be a very useful gadget to help complete the whipping-on of a rod ring. The peg can be used to hold in place a loop of fine but reasonably strong monofilament line, over which the coils of the whipping are made. Then, when it is time to finish the binding, the free end of the whipping line can be passed through the loop of monofilament. A steady pull on this will draw the whipping silk securely and neatly under the binding, which is then complete.

YOUR OWN PLUGS AND LURES

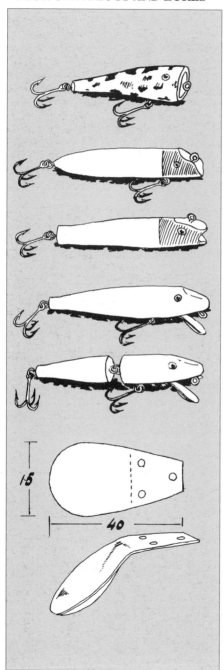

There is great satisfaction in catching a fish on a lure that you, the angler, have designed and crafted yourself. This is not an uncommon achievement among fly-fishers for trout, but it can also be done with other lures.

Wagglers, diving plugs and suchlike lures come in many shapes, sizes, colours and with various actions in the water. The individual lure-maker can apply his own ideas to their design and construction. The examples illustrated here are only some of the most commonly available in tackle shops.

For most freshwater conditions, lengths can be in the range 8–12 cm (3.1–4.7 in), with diameters of 15–25 mm (0.6–1 in). The all-important metal blade that imparts the diving action can be cut from a sheet of brass or aluminium, and the final shape made with a small ball-peen hammer. Spray paints are good for body colour, and the quick-drying ones allow several coats to be applied in fairly quick succession.

VARNISHING A ROD

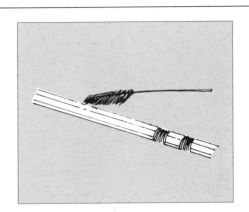

If your rod has blemishes, scratches or scuff marks on its varnish, they can be touched up with a feather or a artist's fine paintbrush, with just a tiny drop of varnish on the tip.

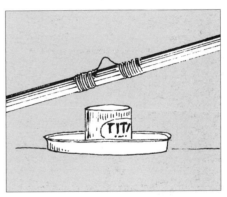

If you wish to re-varnish an entire rod, it is well worth considering a matt varnish. This will prevent bright reflections off your rod, which can frighten fish. Most good varnish goes on smoothly if it is first warmed gently by standing the tin in a container of hot water.

REVIVING YOUR FLIES

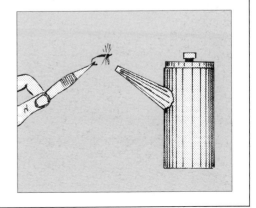

The flies you used last season can be refreshed, restored to their correct shape and generally improved if they are exposed for a few moments to the steam from a boiling kettle or coffee pot. Grasp each fly in tweezers and hold it in the plume of vapour with your hand safely out of the way.

READY FOR TROUTING?

In the very early days of a new season, trout may be slow to come to a fly, and your time may be better spent in making those important last-minute checks of your tackle. This will ensure you are fully equipped and ready to make the most of your chances when the season begins in earnest.

REEL SPOOLS

Any reel that is used hard and regularly tends to collect a certain amount of dirt and grit, which can be damaging to the line and the reel's moving parts. Strip the line off, clean the spool well and lightly oil the moving parts. Then apply a very slight coating of wax to the spool before winding the line back onto it.

RENEWING ROD RINGS

When rod rings have to be replaced or renewed, it is important that the whipping silk is applied with a steady tension. A handy trick for this is to have the silk pass through the leaves of a heavy book, which will apply weight and tension to the silk while allowing it to pull through steadily. When finally varnished, the completed job will look very professional.

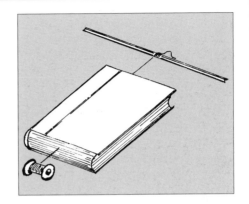

When whipping a ring onto the rod, it makes sense to secure one leg with a temporary turn or two of sticky tape until the whipping of the other leg has been completed. This makes it easier to achieve an absolutely correct ring alignment, and to make slight final adjustments.

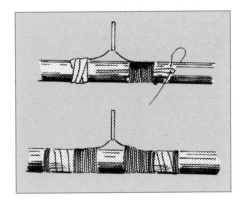

The legs of a ring should be shaped or filed so that they taper and feather into the line of the rod. When wrapped over with whipping silk, the finished profile should be smooth and free of lumps and bumps.

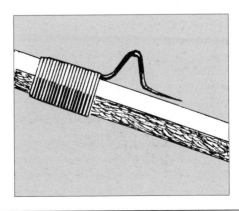

CLEANING THE LINE

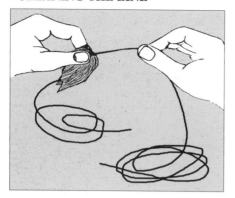

Coiled on a reel or spool, a fishing line is an obvious trap for dirt and damp. A gentle wash in soapy water will remove most of this, and refresh your line's colour and brightness. To finish the job, wipe the line down and dry it by running it through a chamois leather, as shown here.

TUBES FOR RODS

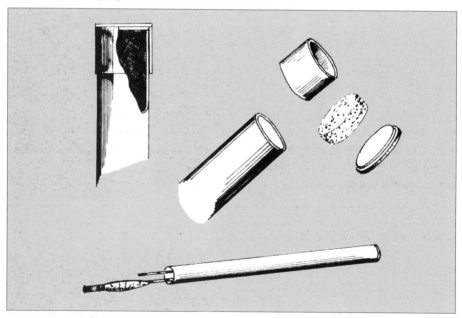

It is a simple job to make a rigid protective case for your rods, using a length of PVC tubing about 50–75 mm (2–3 in) in diameter. Such tubing is widely used by electrical contractors and plumbers, and the best type has a screw-on cap. Others have a press-on end cap. Cut the tubing to length and place a pad of foam or sponge in the cap to absorb hard knocks.

STORING YOUR RODS

Do you store your rods neatly or just pile them in a cupboard? Rods can be stored conveniently and safely by placing them upright in cardboard, synthetic or metal tubes. The first two types can be taped together, and the metal ones soldered. Store the rods in tubes of a suitable diameter, neither too tight nor too large.

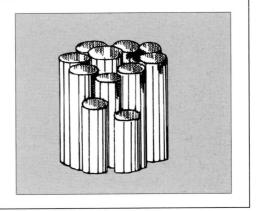

THE TIP RING

The tip ring is subjected to more wear than any of the others. Check it regularly and carefully to avoid it breaking or cracking unexpectedly.

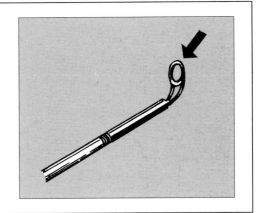

IDENTIFYING YOUR LINES

A small self-adhesive sticker on the back of reel spools can be used to record the details of a line's strength or weight, and to remind you how long it has been there.

8lb
March
1998

A SNUG-FITTING FLY-ROD HANDLE

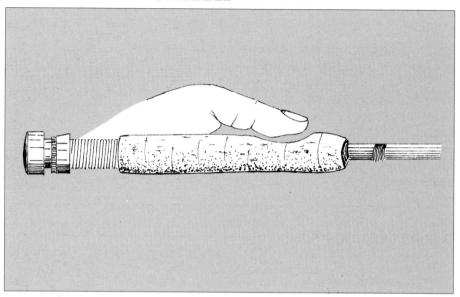

Careful application of a rasp or sandpaper can improve the contours of your rod handle to give a more comfortable and ergonomically suitable shape. This diagram shows just one example of how this can be achieved.

FERRULE ADJUSTMENT

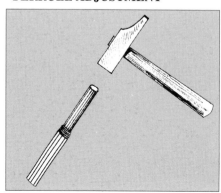

If the metal ferrules of your rod are rather slack, various methods can be used to tighten them. A simple technique is shown here, and involves tapping very gently with a small hammer on the end of the male ferrule, until it has been flattened enough to give the required tightness of fit.

CARING FOR RODS

It is all too easy to transport rods on the back shelf of your car. But this can subject them to damagingly high temperatures on sunny days, even when it is quite cool outside. Weakening or warping may well result. It is also not a suitable place to put your camera equipment. Both should be stored where it is cooler and darker.

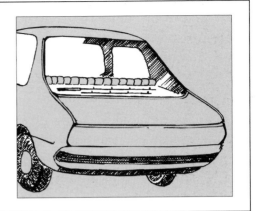

FERRULE LUBRICATION

If the female ferrule of a rod becomes dry and inclined to stick, it can be cleaned and lightly lubricated using cotton buds, available from any pharmacy. Stubborn dirt can be removed with a bud soaked in surgical spirit or alcohol.

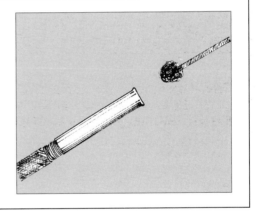

DON'T LOSE YOUR CAPS!

This diagram shows a simple and effective way to make sure you don't lose the caps of your rod tubes. All it requires is two buttons, one on either end of a length of stout mono-filament line, which is threaded through a hole in the cap and the rod tube.

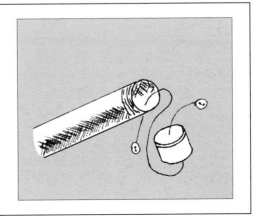

MARK YOUR REEL

Reels are valuable. It is therefore a good idea to mark them clearly with your name and telephone number, either with an indelible marker or by having the reel engraved. If you should lose a reel and it is found by some honest person, you may be reunited with it quite quickly.

DRYING OUT FLIES

Flies that are damp should never be left in a closed box. At the end of a day's fishing it is worth leaving your box open in an airy and warm place, so that the dampness evaporates. You thereby minimise the risk of hooks becoming rusted and weakened.

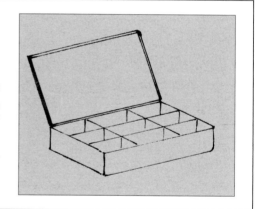

WELL-FITTED WADERS

Your correct foot size is not the only thing to look for when buying a new pair of waders. Freedom of movement is important, too, and you should be able to raise and bend each leg quite freely. The diagram shows a simple test that you can carry out in the tackle shop, to ensure that the waders will bend and flex sufficiently.

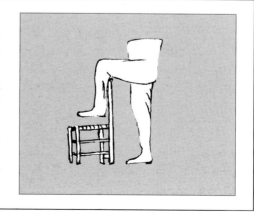

FIXED-SPOOL REELS

If the drag of your fixed-spool reel has a tendency to work loose, the threads can be tightened up by coating the inside with a light coat of varnish. This should provide a little more resistance, and prevent the spool working loose when it is in use.

ROD ALIGNMENT MARKS

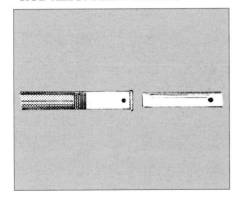

It is essential that the sections of a rod are put together so that all the rings are correctly aligned. One helpful way of ensuring this is to paint a small marker on the male and female ferrules of each joint. If these witness marks are correctly positioned when the rod if put up, everything should be in perfect alignment.

KEEPING HOOKS IN ORDER

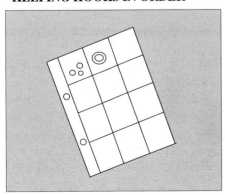

A good way to sort hooks into handy little batches according to size and type is to use a clear plastic sheet with separate little pockets, like those used by stamp and coin collectors. You can see the contents clearly, and each pocket can also be marked.

TAKING RODS DOWN

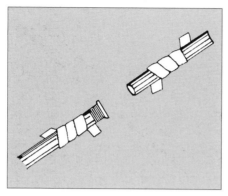

A good way to make a rod joint easy to pull apart is to glue a small strip of rubber cut from an old inner tube close to each ferrule, as shown here. This gives a good grip, and the sections should come apart with a firm, steady pulling and twisting movement.

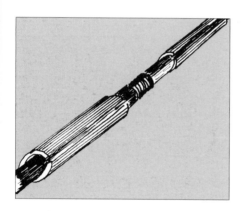

Another good way to get a firm, non-slip grip on two rod sections is to slip on two split lengths of rubber tubing of a suitable diameter, one above and one below the joint.

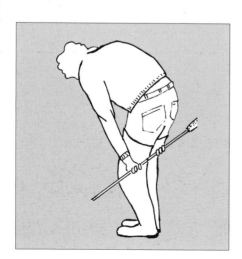

At the end of a long day's fishing, it is always a nuisance to discover that two rod sections are firmly stuck. The diagram shows a tip for tackling this problem without tools or equipment. Hold the rod behind your legs at knee height, and pull steadily. If your hands are dry, this should enable you to pull hard without twisting or bending the rod dangerously.

MARKING YOUR ROD-CASE

When travelling by rail or air, it is a good idea to mark your rod-cases or tubes prominently with turns of distinctively coloured tape. When claiming your baggage, this helps you to distinguish your own tubes from other people's.

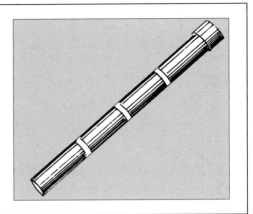

BOOT-HANGER

Boots and waders are best dried out and stored by hanging them as shown. A convenient hanger can be made by twisting and bending a length of 4–5 mm (0.16–0.2 in) diameter wire into this shape, and it may also be possible to make one out of a heavy-gauge wire coat-hanger.

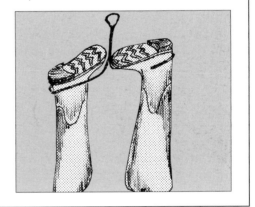

HOOKS

Hooks come with many subtle but important differences of shape, length and gape (barbed and barbless etc). Carry a good selection of different types, keep them separate and clearly marked, and choose your hook with care for each angling situation.

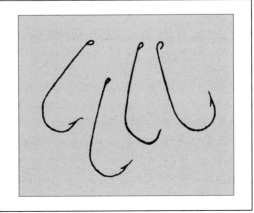

10. ACCESSORIES AND GADGETS

HAND-LINE FRAMES

If you are making a frame to hold a hand-line, it is a good idea to have quite broad side-pieces. These will stand out above the level of the wound-on line, and give some protection to floats, hooks and other bits of equipment.

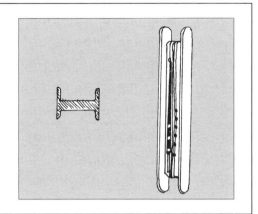

MARKING LINES

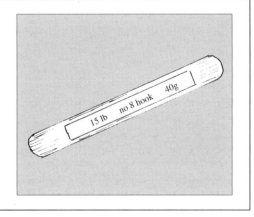

When hand-lines are stored on frames, it is a good idea to mark the line's details on the side of the frame.

HOOK REMOVER

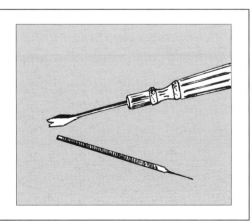

A handy hook remover can be made by using a triangular file to cut a V-shaped notch in the blade of an old screwdriver. Once the notch is engaged with the hook, pressure can be applied to free it quite easily.

GAFF

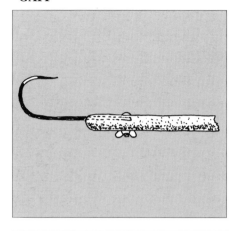

Gaffs and landing-hooks (now largely confined to sea fishing from boats) can be awkward and hazardous things to transport. This first diagram shows how the hook can be attached and removed from the shaft by using a bolt and wing-nut.

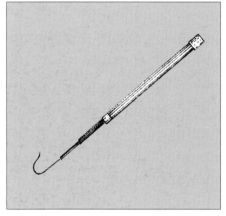

A gaff of the correct length is essential, but a long one can be awkward. A telescopic type allows a short and easily handled gaff to be extended quickly.

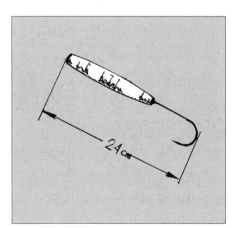

A short-handled gaff has its uses when pike fishing, and a fish neatly gaffed through the lower jaw can usually be released unharmed if desired. The diagram shows a short freshwater gaff made with the handle of a discarded rod.

ROD RACK

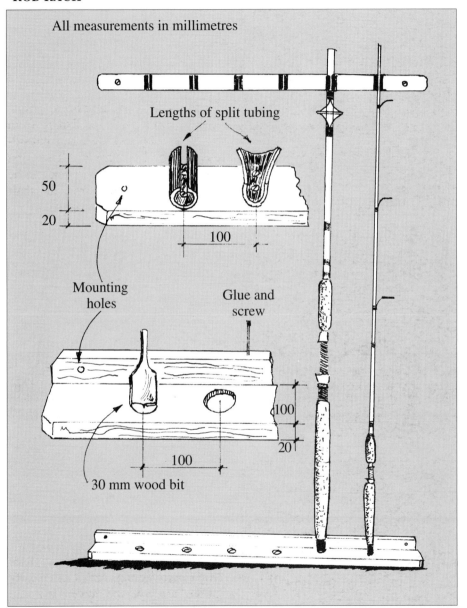

All measurements in millimetres

Lengths of split tubing

50
20
100

Mounting holes

Glue and screw

30 mm wood bit

100
20
100

This diagram shows how easily a rod rack can be made. All that is required is some wood, a saw, a drill and wood bits, a length of plastic tubing, and some screws and glue.

REEL FITTINGS

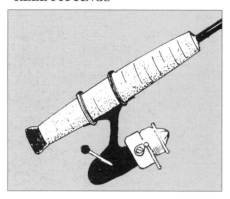

With time and use, a rod's original reel fittings can become loose. They can be quickly reinforced or even replaced by bands cut from the inner tube of a bicycle tyre. The inner tube's diameter should be less than that of the rod handle.

ANGLER'S TORCH

For night fishing, and even towards dusk, a small torch is important. Only a small battery-powered unit is required, and if it can be pinned or hooked onto the angler's jacket or vest, it leaves both hands free.

STORING LURES

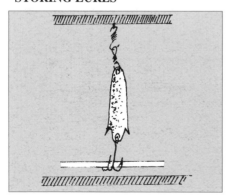

The diagram shows how lures can be stored in an orderly way, without getting entangled. Here, the hook is held by a strip of soft wood, and a small spring goes into the eye of the swivel, to hold the lure out straight.

MODIFIED FLOAT

This is an easy way to modify a float so that it can run freely on a line, with a split shot acting as a stop. Heat the upper plastic stem and flatten it at the end. Then use a fine-pointed implement to bore a small hole through the centre of the flattened end.

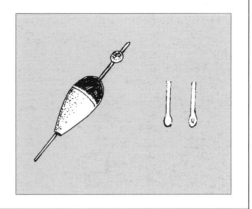

PIKE GAGS

No-one wants to get bitten or torn by the many razor-sharp teeth of a pike, so a pike-gag of heavy-duty, springy wire is a useful gadget. It is a good idea to use one that is covered in a brightly coloured plastic coating, as shown in the upper drawing. If you drop it, it is easy to see and recover. To prevent snagging in your pocket or bag, the sharp points can be protected by slipping short lengths of rubber tubing over them.

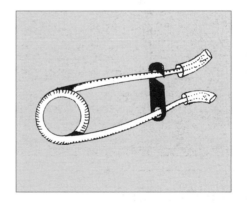

It may not be necessary to remove these protective rubber pieces, as the gag will probably work quite effectively and is less likely to damage a fish you wish to return, compared with the harshness of the traditional gag shown in the lower drawing.

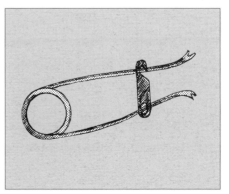

FLOATS

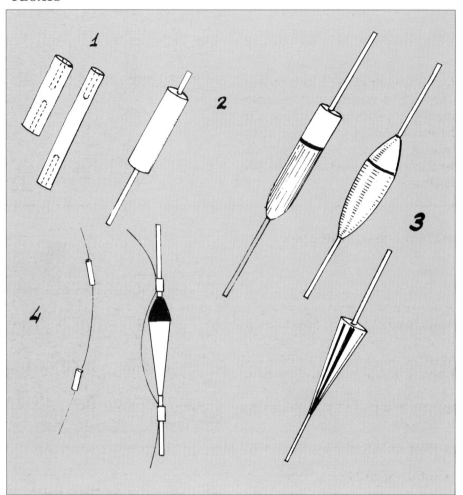

It is useful to have a selection of floats that can be quickly changed without having to take your line and terminal tackle to pieces. Balsa wood is buoyant, easy to shape and cut, and is the best material.

1. Cut balsa doweling to the required length and drill both ends.
2. Using epoxy glue, fix a stem in the top and bottom.
3. Carve the balsa into shape, and paint and varnish it to your chosen colours.
4. Two pieces of thin rubber tubing threaded on the line will allow firm fixing of the floats, and easy changing.

COATED MATCHES

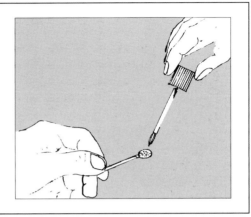

Matches are useless if they get wet. They can be waterproofed by applying a fine coating of nail varnish or lacquer to the match head. It is always a good idea to have a box of weatherproofed matches in your fishing box or jacket.

AUDIBLE BITE INDICATOR

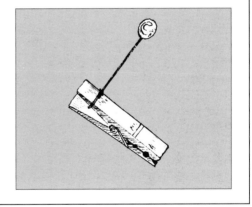

A wooden or plastic clothes-peg to which a small bell has been attached by a stiff wire, makes a simple but effective audible bite indicator. The longer the length of wire used to mount the bell, the more sensitive it will be. The peg attaches the gadget to the rod.

USEFUL NEEDLE

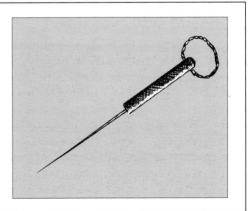

A fine-pointed needle set into a simple wooden handle will have countless uses when you are fishing, including clearing the eyes of flies and other hooks, and helping to undo tiny and stubborn knots. A cork or suchlike can be used to protect the point, when not in use.

KEEPER-RING

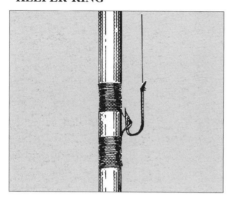

Nowadays, most rods are made with a small ring whipped in place just forward of the handle, into which the angler can hook his fly or single hook, or one leg of a double or treble. If you have a rod that lacks this keeper-ring, you can easily add one. A whip-finish, varnished when the job is complete, is best.

PINCERS

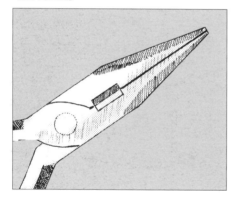

Fine-nosed pincers or pliers are extremely useful for all kinds of little angling tasks. It is almost impossible to bend deformed hooks back into shape without them, to mention just one example of their many uses. If a long string or lanyard is fastened to one of the handles, it will safeguard against accidental loss.

HANDY ABRASIVE

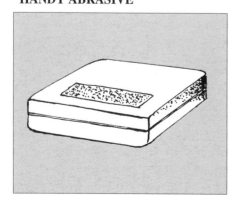

A small patch of fine sandpaper or glass paper, glued onto the top of a fly- or lure-box, comes in handy when it is necessary to touch up the point of a blunted hook, or to give a brightly-burnished finish to the blade of a spinning lure that has become dull.

BALL-BEARING SWIVELS

Swivels with a ball-bearing mechanism tend to be among the most expensive on the market, and are not available in very small sizes. But for sea fishing, and for large freshwater species such as pike, they are by far the best, and will keep a line from kinking even when there is a lot of pressure on it.

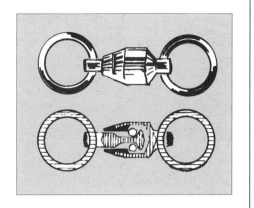

MULTI-PURPOSE FISHING BAG

A fishing bag is not only for your spare tackle. Try to choose (or make) one that will hold both the fish you have caught, keeping them well ventilated and fresh, and carry your picnic lunch. Try to choose a fishing bag that will also carry a camera to record your successes, especially the fish that you return. But do not make it too bulky or heavy.

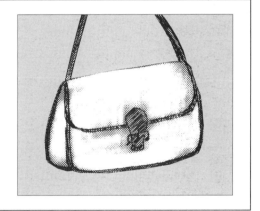

NAIL CLIPPERS

A small set of nail clippers is the perfect tool for cutting monofilament, and especially for trimming loose ends after tying a knot. Another advantage, of course, is that they can be used with one hand. A line or loop of cord passed through the eye will reduce your chances of losing them.

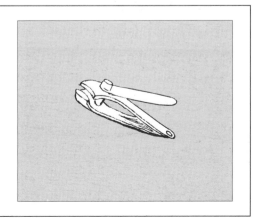

USES FOR A CAMERA FILM HOLDER

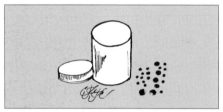

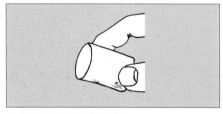

The handy little plastic pots that 35 mm camera film come in can be used for many purposes. They make good containers to keep matches dry, and when the cap has been pierced with little holes, they will keep live insects and small invertebrates in good condition. They also make good containers for small quantities of instant coffee, dried milk and other picnic essentials.

Many little items, such as hooks, shot, small baits and even aspirins and anti-histamine tablets can be stored in them – provided the contents are labelled clearly and correctly! A camera film pot can be used to hold a stub of candle for emergencies, and if you need to wash your hands at the end of a day's fishing, they will hold just the right quantity of soap or detergent liquid. A quantity of floatant, home-made or shop-bought, can be kept in a film pot, and a dry fly dunked in it as required. The possible uses for these extremely handy little containers is inexhaustible.

FISHING JOURNAL

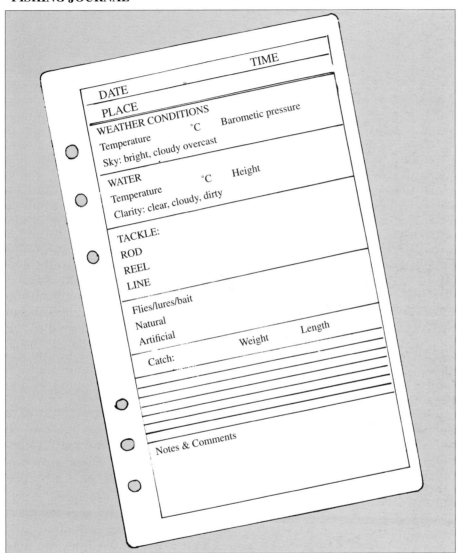

Each individual angler may wish to have his own personal diary layout, to record the events and conditions of a day's fishing. But here is one possible format that covers most of the essentials; and you can modify it to suit your personal preferences. However you may do it, it is always well worth keeping a detailed fishing diary.

SAFETY-PIN HINT

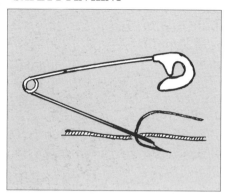

If you have the misfortune to get a hook stuck in your finger, use a safety-pin to remove it. After sterilising the point in a flame, push the pin gently into the wound, parallel to the hook point. Once it is past the barb, hold it firmly in place and steadily withdraw the hook and the pin together. The hook should come out smoothly and without tearing.

SOME SIMPLE TOOLS

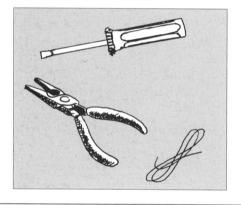

Never set off without a few simple tools and repair materials – they may save the day from disaster. Take a small screwdriver, a pair of pincers, some fine wire, some sticky tape etc. If you do not need them yourself, some fellow-angler may benefit from them.

MAKESHIFT WADING STAFF

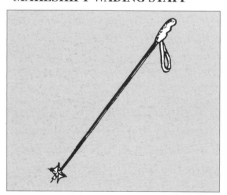

A cast-off ski-stick can serve as a good wading staff in waters where the current is fast and you need to probe ahead for hidden snags and potholes. Keep it in your car, so it will be there if you need it.

A WATERPROOF IN YOUR BAG

Wherever and whenever you go fishing, rain is always a possibility. There should be room in your fishing bag or creel for a lightweight rainproof, which you can bundle up tightly with a couple of rubber bands, and stow away until needed.

SAFETY-PIN TACKLE HOLDER

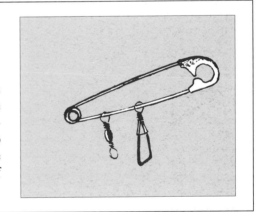

Tiny bits and pieces, such as swivels and other items with eyes, can be kept securely and neatly on a safety-pin. It is a quick and simple job to take off what you need, without the need to rummage in the corners of your pockets.

KNOT FOR ROD RINGS

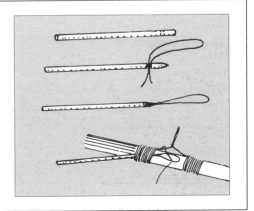

The whip-finish is used for attaching rings to fishing rods of every kind. Finishing this very neat binding is easier if you can make a simple tool with a loop of monofilament, as shown in the diagram, to draw the silk back under the turns of the whipping.

CHEAP AND CHEERFUL ANCHOR

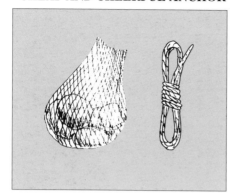

When fishing from a smallish boat, a makeshift anchor can be put together easily by taking a mesh bag, as used for fruit and suchlike, and filling it with stones. Make sure the bag is sound, and lash it to the boat's painter or other mooring point with a good strong length of rope.

HOME-MADE DISGORGER

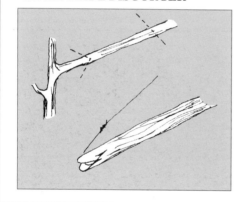

If you need a disgorger but do not have one with you, here is how to make one quickly with just a length of twig and a knife. A dry piece of twig may be harder, but avoid using a dry and brittle piece of wood.

SCISSOR-POINT PROTECTION

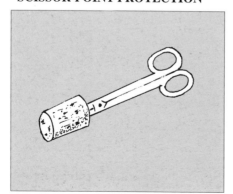

A pair of fine-pointed scissors are extremely useful as part of your gear, but their delicate points should be protected from accidental damage by placing a cork over them when they are not in use.

ARTERY FORCEPS

Artery or haemostatic forceps, as used in surgery, can be lock closed and have many uses for the fisherman as a 'third hand'. If you can't obtain them from a doctor friend, they are widely and cheaply available from pharmacies and medical equipment suppliers.

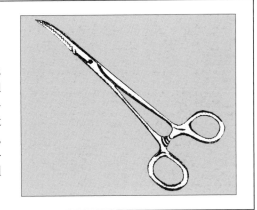

BITE INDICATORS

If you do not want to invest in the latest electronic bite indicators, other more traditional options are available. One of the oldest and most widely used is a little bell attached to the rod, as shown here, preferably somewhere in the upper third of its length.

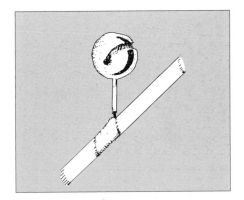

A short length of plastic tubing, cut as illustrated here, can be a very sensitive and useful bite indicator. If it is placed over a stick in the water, even a very gentle bite will send it shooting upwards to show a fish has taken.

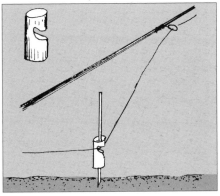

FLOAT FOR WINDY DAYS

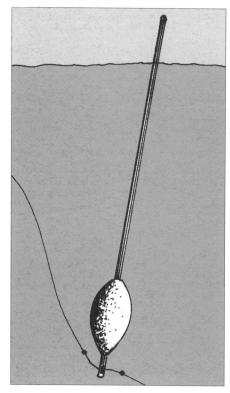

When float fishing in windy conditions, a conventional float may cause too much surface disturbance or agitation to the bait as the breeze catches it. This problem can be largely overcome by using a float like the one in this diagram. The weight is at the bottom of the float, and only a slender tip is exposed above the surface.

ROD REST

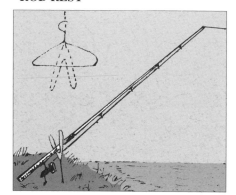

A wire coat-hanger covered in plastic can quickly be modified as shown in the diagram, to make a handy little rod rest for times when you are ledgering a bait or fishing on the bottom.

FINDING THE DEPTH

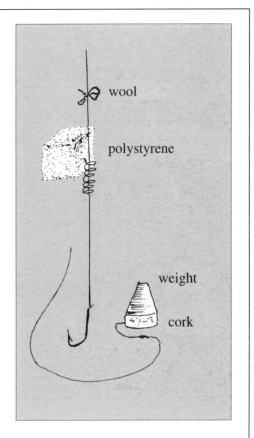

wool

polystyrene

weight

cork

When you want to fish on or close to the bottom, it is essential to know the water's depth. First attach a weight to the line, and then a little free-running float made from a piece of polystyrene, attached to the line by a spiral or wire. If a loosely-knotted piece of wool is tied onto the line above this float, its final position will indicate the depth. Then remove the weight and float, and start fishing!

POLISHING

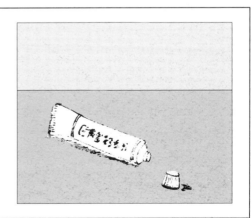

A tube of toothpaste can be useful on a day's fishing. Among other ingredients, it includes an abrasive that can be used to brighten up lures, polish hooks and even help to get the smell of fish off your hands at the end of the day.

SWIVELS

Always use swivels, especially when fishing in fast currents and with rather fine lines, as well as with twirling lures. A line that gets twisted and starts to kink can give rise to many problems and tangles – its life will also be shortened.

11. MISHAPS AND REPAIRS

WATERPROOF PROTECTION

Instant-seal clear plastic envelopes are cheap and extremely useful for keeping documents, fishing permits, cigarettes and many other vulnerable items safe, in the event of very wet conditions or an unexpected tumble into the water.

DISCARDED LINES

Never discard old or unwanted line by the waterside. Monofilament is not biodegradable, and can easily get snagged around boat propellers and on other anglers' tackle. It is also a major hazard for birds and small mammals. Take it home!

HOOKED!

If you have the misfortune to get a hook stuck in a finger or other flesh, do not attempt to pull it out. Try gently to push the point and the barb out, and then cut off both point and barb. It should then be possible to withdraw the remainder of the hook easily. Do not forget to disinfect the wound thoroughly.

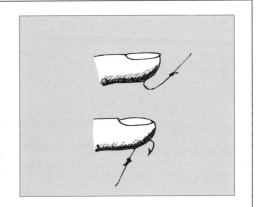

MIDGES

Midges and other small biting insects can sometimes be a dreadful torment to anglers. Various excellent repellent preparations are available in pharmacies, and some should always be carried, especially in warm and humid weather.

PATCHES

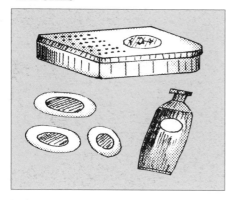

Waders, fishing boots and waterproofs are all vulnerable to punctures and tears, and clothing or footwear that leaks can ruin a day's fishing. A small tin will suffice to hold a selection of patches of various sizes, and some adhesive.

INSULATING TAPE

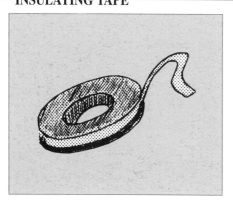

Always carry a roll of PVC insulating tape, as used by electricians. It has innumerable emergency uses: to bind up a rod, to secure a joint, repair a landing-net handle and much, much more.

12. MISCELLANEOUS

DIRECTION-FINDING

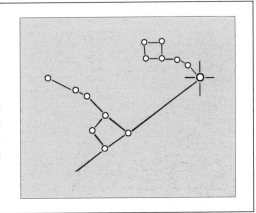

Can you find the Pole Star? It is not difficult, if you extend an imaginary line from the two lower stars of the Ursa Major (Great Bear or the Plough) constellation. At about five times the distance between those two pointers you will see the Pole Star, which indicates north.

THE CONDITION OF FISH

The best way to judge the condition of a dead fish is to examine its eyes. They should be bright and clear, with no cloudiness or filminess. Also, pinch the upper flanks with your fingers. If the impression of your finger and thumb does not disappear almost immediately, the fish has been out of the water for some time.

IMPROVING THE FLAVOUR OF FISH

The muddy taste of carp and certain other freshwater fish is caused by the blueish-green algae on which they feed occasionally, which builds up in their muscles. Such fish can be easily cleared of this unpleasant taste if they are transferred for a few days to a pond that contains clear, algae-free water.

HAKE AND PIKE

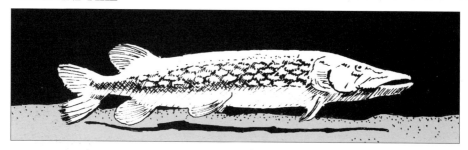

The hake *Merlucius merlucius* takes its Latin name from its supposed resemblance to the freshwater pike, and it was formerly referred to as the 'sea-pike'.

RAINBOWS

A saying from the lips of an old country clergyman: 'A rainbow that appears late in the day foretells fine weather tomorrow'.

STURGEON EGGS

The sturgeon is by far the most prolific egg producer, and a female may carry between 4 and 5 million eggs. Trout and salmon produce about 2000 eggs for each kilo of their body weight. Pike produce about 20,000 to 30,000, and carp and tench between 200,000 and 300,000.

IMPROVISED CUP

You can improvise a cup for a quick drink of water or other beverage by cutting off the top of an empty soup packet. When opened up as shown in this diagram, it makes a perfectly serviceable drinking vessel.

WILD MINT

Wild mint or water mint is often to be found close to the water's edge. Line the bottom of your creel or fish basket with this, and it will impart a fragrant aroma when the fish are cooked. If you cannot find mint, the equally common fennel can be used.

SUNSET TIME

If you want to estimate how long it will be before the sun sets, count how many fingers of your out-stretched hand fill the space between the horizon and the sun. Allow 15 minutes for each finger.

?

FISH SPAWNING

Freshwater fish do not spawn between August and October. From November until as late as February, game fish such as trout and salmon are spawning. Pike begin in March, and most cyprinoid fish in May. Carp and tench spawn in summer. Seasonal weather conditions can affect spawning dates, but seldom by more than a fortnight. If game fish are out of season between November and March, why are pike not protected between February and April?

THE TROUT BREEDING CYCLE

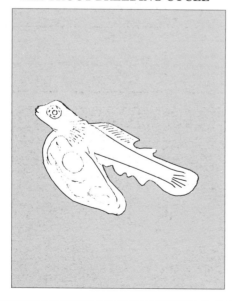

Trout begin their cycle of reproduction in the autumn. The female uses powerful movements of her body and tail to excavate a small depression in the gravel, in which she lays her eggs. The male fertilises them, and the pair cover them up. The eggs' development is dictated by the water temperature, taking a month at 10°C. The newly hatched alevins first absorb the yolk sac from which they draw nourishment. After about a fortnight they seek out hiding places, and swim freely in search of food.

THE ANGLER'S PRAYER

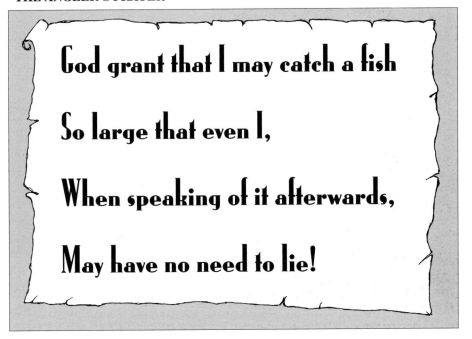

God grant that I may catch a fish

So large that even I,

When speaking of it afterwards,

May have no need to lie!

The angler's prayer is an earnest wish that, some day, the truth will be an adequate substitute for the typical exaggeration of fishermen.

A FISHY SMELL

Even if you have washed your hands at the waterside, some fishy smell usually lingers. The best way of getting rid of this is to use bicarbonate of soda in place of soap, or to use a mixture of the two.

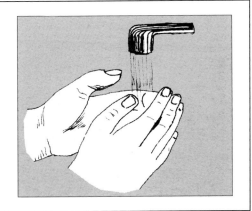

WEATHER FORECASTING

When you see distant flashes of lightning coming towards you, if you move northwards or north-westwards it is very possible that you will encounter the storm. But if you move south or west, you may avoid it altogether.

If you are setting off early to go fishing, and wondering whether or not to burden yourself with a waterproof coat, a simple trick is to examine the grass. If it is dry, it is highly likely that it will rain during the day.

THE SPEED OF FISH

The speed at which fish swim is determined by their caudal fins (i.e. tail), which provide the driving force. The other fins chiefly provide direction and stability. The sleekest and most streamlined fish are the fastest. The speed of various species have been measured in metres per second : salmon 8, trout 4, pike 0.45, carp 0.4. The record is held by the red tuna, at 10 kilometres per hour (6.2 mph).

THE SMALL SPOON LURE

A French angling book of 1907 declares 'the spoon bait is a simple and almost infallible lure. As its name indicates, the essential part is a small coffee spoon with the handle cut off. Some people are content with an iron spoon, or one of silver-plated copper, while others use solid silver. The spoon should have a treble hook at one end and at the other, smaller, end the line is attached by a swivel or split ring.'

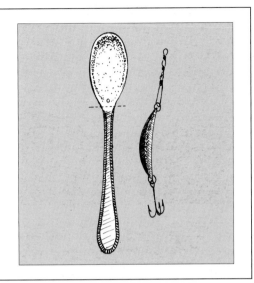

VIBERT BOX

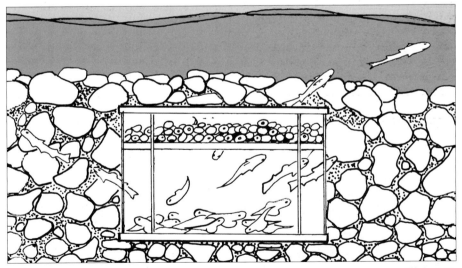

A Vibert box or cage is simply a small plastic container measuring about 140 × 60 × 85 mm (5.5 × 2.4 × 3.3 in)and containing around 500 eyed trout ova. It is used to restock a stretch of water. The eggs are safe from predators; the alevins do not have to swim actively until they have absorbed their yolk sacs; and as the little trout emerge they will gradually take to living just as freely and successfully as their wild cousins.

?

Notes

Notes

Notes

Notes

Notes